I0813391

GIVE CLUTTER THE MIDDLE FINGER

GIVE CLUTTER THE MIDDLE FINGER

A CHINGONA'S GUIDE TO TAKING CONTROL OF YOUR STUFF AND YOUR LIFE

MEGGIE MANGIONE

Any product names, logos, brands, and other trademarks featured or referred to in this book are the property of their respective trademark holders. Neither the author nor publisher are affiliated, associated, authorized, endorsed by, or in any way officially connected with such trademark holders.

Published by Greenleaf Book Group Press
Austin, Texas
www.gbgpress.com

Distributed by Greenleaf Book Group

For ordering information or special discounts for bulk purchases, please contact Greenleaf Book Group at PO Box 91869, Austin, TX 78709, 512.891.6100.

Design and composition by Greenleaf Book Group and Teresa Muñiz
Cover design by Greenleaf Book Group and Teresa Muñiz
Cover photo by Brianne Thomas, Little BeeLoved Photography
Photographs on pages xii, 14, 38, 54, 66, 71, 86, 98, 101, 138, 147, 152, 232 by Brianne Thomas, Little BeeLoved Photography
Photographs on pages 10, 94, 133, 158, 159, 169, 170, 219, 225 by Colleen Scott Hartel, Colleen Scott Photography
Photographs on pages 24, 91, 184, 185, 208 by Dani Williams, Dani and Daniel Photography
Photograph on page 240 by Stacy Sikes

Publisher's Cataloging-in-Publication data is available.

Print ISBN: 979-8-88645-252-5

eBook ISBN: 979-8-88645-253-2

To offset the number of trees consumed in the printing of our books, Greenleaf donates a portion of the proceeds from each printing to the Arbor Day Foundation. Greenleaf Book Group has replaced over 50,000 trees since 2007.

Printed in the United States of America on acid-free paper

25 26 27 28 29 30 31 10 9 8 7 6 5 4 3 2 1

First Edition

CONTENTS

CHAPTER TWO

CHAPTER THREE

CHAPTER FOUR

CHAPTER FIVE

CHAPTER SIX

CHAPTER SEVEN

Jonathan James and the Whatif Monster
Michelle Nelson-Schmidt
Kane Miller
romeo & juliet
GIBBS SMITH
Yolen & Teague
How Do Dinosaurs Say Happy Birthday?
BLUE SKY PRESS
My Rules for Being a Pretty Princess
Heath McKenzie
Mayer
Staying Overnight
GOLDEN
LEVEL 1
A NEW FRIEND
Mike Wu
ELLIE
Disney · HYPERION
SESAME STREET
LET'S LEARN ABOUT - THE HUMAN BODY
bendon
Meltzer · Eliopoulos
I am Abraham Lincoln
Dial
Go, Dog. Go!
P. D. Eastman
Brown
Hurd
GOODNIGH
THRIFTBOOKS
H. A. REY
CURIOUS GEORGE
H. M. CO.
First Words ENGLISH-SPANISH
Primeras palabras ESPAÑOL-INGLÉS
Award
LOMP
MAMASAURUS
chronicle books
Willems
An ELEPHANT & PIGGIE Book
I WILL TAKE A NAP!
HYPERION DBG
Willems
An ELEPHANT & PIGGIE Book
A BIG GUY TOOK MY BALL!
HYPERION DBG
Viorst/Cruz
ALEXANDER AND THE TERRIBLE, HORRIBLE, NO GOOD, VERY BAD DAY
Atheneum
Dean
Pete the Cat Meet Pete
HARPER

willems The Pigeon Finds a Hot Dog! hyperion/dbg
willems The Pigeon Needs a Bath! hyperion/dbg
willems Don't Let the Pigeon Drive the Bus! hyperion/dbg
willems The Pigeon Wants a Puppy! hyperion dbg
All Better! Henning Löhlein • Bernd Penners Kane Miller EDC PUBLISHING
Dean Pete the Cat Big Easter Adventure HARPER
LEVEL 3 GREEN LIGHT READERS EGAN DODSWORTH IN NEW YORK
NOISY DINOSAURS tiger tales
Numeroff/Bond If You Give a Moose a Muffin Weekly Reader Books
Good Morning, Good Night Buenos días, buenas noches A Touch & Feel Bedtime Book Bilingual Edition Piggy Toes PRESS
RINKER • LICHTENHELD Mighty, Mighty Construction Site
BEGINNER BOOKS THE CAT IN THE HAT Dr. Seuss B-1
Musical Nativity Illustrated by Alida Massari Usborne
Willems AN ELEPHANT & PIGGIE Book WAITING IS NOT EASY! HYPERION DBG
An I Can Read Book AMELIA BEDELIA Parish / Siebel HarperTrophy
REY CURIOUS GEORGE FLIES A KITE Weekly Reader Books
Schertle McElmurry El camioncito Azul HMH
FRANCESCA PESKIN

INTRODUCTION

This is not a book filled with pretty pictures and lists of unrealistic expectations. Most of us are in the thick of schedules packed to the brim and responsibilities wrapping around the corner. I'm not here to shame you about the clutter you're living with, but rather to help you ease your way into a *less* cluttered life. This is a book to reprogram the stigma and judgment we have about clutter, reshape the goal of what being organized really feels and looks like, and ultimately stop letting clutter control our emotions and the evaluation of our self-worth.

All the perfectly edited photos we see on home décor profiles and interior design sites that seem void of "normalcy" are intended to inspire, yet I believe for a lot of us they simply make us feel less than—failures in the way we manage our homes and our lives. I have been in hundreds and hundreds of homes, and I am here to pull back the curtain on how most people really live, and in comparison, to shed light on how professional organizers really live as well.

At my first national professional organizer convention, I sat in a room with a few hundred people—mostly women, most of them older than I was. I was in my first few years of business and hadn't been able to afford to attend before, so this was my inauguration. During this time, I had only one child, who was a young toddler, and we lived in two upstairs bedrooms at my mother's house while saving up to buy a house. What little we owned and used fit in the two rooms, and what didn't was neatly packed in a small storage unit. Little time was needed for chores because of the small square footage, and budget prevented new items from showing up.

At the convention, one of the opening speakers made a comment about how ironic it would be if a client could see inside our own homes, and the audience roared with laughter. I didn't understand the inside joke, yet almost everyone was laughing. That moment struck me, the bright-eyed and bushy-tailed novice: Were we not the professionals who kept a pristine home as an example of our expertise? How little experience I had at the time running my own household with growing kids and hobbies while working full time outside the home, and how ironic that my clients would end up more organized than I did.

One of the biggest misconceptions about my life as a

professional organizer is the belief that my home must look like the pages of a lifestyle magazine. People believe the rooms of my abode could be likened to a spread in *Better Homes & Gardens* or *House Beautiful*, in that I have everything neatly put away at all times. Everything has a place, there are no unidentified piles of junk, and everything is polished and ready for a close-up. And why wouldn't you think that? While I love my homegirl Martha Stewart, she is the one who ignited this trend of organized home idealism in the '80s with her books and magazines, along with a slew of other homemaking professionals. We could go as far back as the 1950s with the idealism of the nuclear families and the roles of women, which often included creating a neatly coiffed homestead. Thanks, Mrs. Cleaver.

Almost every book on organizing your home is littered with perfectly staged images of interior spaces, making you believe that the task of getting organized is a finite point you reach: if you do ALL the things listed on the pages—which is expressed to be as basic and easy as snapping your fingers—you will be organized and your home will stay that way forever. Don't blame this messenger, but that's an untrue depiction of an organized journey. The number you have dialed has been disconnected.

To be fair, this idealistic perfectionism is easy to sell. Who doesn't want to live in a house that looks as though it was professionally designed with the latest trends and is also as clean and organized as a fresh hotel room? In this type of space, there are no chores beckoning our attention, no piles of laundry calling for our time. The to-do list is absent because it's all done. Sounds awesome; where do we sign up? And this is where the thread unravels.

It's not real life—the part of real life where we're rushing from event to event, from work to activities, and leaving behind a tornado path of destruction through our spaces. There's minimal honesty about the struggles each of us faces on a daily basis just to make sure everyone in our house has clean underwear. We are expected to jump from "does everyone have clean underwear" to a magazine spread in a matter of 150 pages.

I am obsessed with organizing. I am type A, professionally diagnosed perfectionist with a touch of OCD, and a first-born daughter—my interest in organizing was embedded in my DNA. My obsession is in the pursuit of being organized and being as efficient as possible, yet I also feel the pressure and struggle to maintain an organized life. That is the reason I'm here with you right now, writing this book, because I'm next to you saying, "Babe, me too!" *I get it.* So let's share a chuckle of relief, tweak the goal to something realistic, and take the first step together.

First order of business: the standards have to change. I want to be a voice of vulnerability in this industry and tell you I'm not giving up all standards, but I am also not going to continue carrying anxiety because my home isn't as perfect as those pictures. Living life to the fullest can be messy, so why are we surprised that most homes are messy? I often travel throughout the year, which means luggage and laundry in rotation. I pursue my goals fiercely, such as writing this book and maintaining a consistently healthy lifestyle, which equates to time not spent doing chores. When relaxation is needed, I push guilt aside and put my feet up to spend time with my spouse and kids. Downtime is essential to keep burnout at bay.

For too long we have let our clutter control our environment and even our stress level. Clutter intrudes on our freedom to live life to the fullest. I'll go back to school . . . start salsa lessons . . . host friends over for bunco when . . . the house is put back together again. Here's the thing, Humpty Dumpty: it's not gonna be put back together again in the way you're imagining as long as you are living life in it. Those social media brags with the spotless house are either devout minimalists or have tons of outside help, or, the most likely scenario—they're showing you what they want you to see but not the full story (the piles are hidden in cabinets and drawers). So how is it possible to ease the reins on expectations without criticizing our worth? This is made possible by shifting to a healthy relationship with stuff, adjusting expectations, and becoming a more realistic version of organized-ish.

Now let's squelch the belief of professional organizers living in this alternate universe of a house without clutter. Do you also imagine that every restaurant chef makes themselves a three-course meal each evening after 10 long hours in a hot kitchen? I'd be willing to bet that outside of family dinner on the clock at the restaurant, even a Michelin-star homie is poppin' a package of ramen or a boring baked potato on an off day. It doesn't discredit their dedication to their craft or how amazing they are at their job. It means they're humans, not robots, and they aren't paying themselves top dollar for a gourmet lunch.

Do you suppose every nutritionist skips every sweet that passes by their face, too? You know as well as I do that there's a bowl of ice cream or a donut that doesn't get entered into the food diary every week. What about all the doctors you encounter? Are they in peak athletic condition, since they can't seem to tell us enough about working out 30 minutes five times a week or drinking so much water we feel bloated? Medical professionals have all the access to the latest health studies and yet also struggle with obesity, addictions, and finding time to hit the gym—just like the rest of us. I even had a conversation with my dear sweet angel housekeeper, who is my favorite person to whom I'm not related. She and I talked about how tough it is to do, in our own homes, the thing we spend the majority of the week doing for others in their homes. She's tired by the weekend, and after cleaning five to six houses per week, adding her own house to the list is low on the priority list. We have commiserated on this frustrating reality and ended with *oh well, fuck it* (but in Spanish).

Here's the truth: I live in the same crazy, never-stop-moving world that you do. My schedule stays packed. I'm grateful to have business opportunities, my kids have never-ending activities, and I still make time for myself every single day in ways that do not include house chores. Included in my personal universe is a pack of mess-makers I lovingly refer to as my family. This is real life for everyone from A-list celebrities to the teacher and police officer newlywed couple starting their life together. When we accept this reality as normal and come to terms with the fact that it's not going to change, like ever, then we can start to do the real work on our hearts, manage our expectations, and make a realistic and achievable plan.

Need another reality check to convince you? Remember in 2020 when the world got fucking canceled? COVID brought an end to everything on your schedule. No school—for the first time ever, we pulled the plug on education with no real plan. No work (for some of us)—most of my team was on unemployment while I burned through savings because unemployment doesn't cover business owners. No social calendar, no dinner dates, no traveling, no nothing. We had absolutely no plans outside of essential workers.

As it turns out, having time to get organized was in fact not the mountain stopping you from succeeding. My team and I panicked, sure as day that everyone would figure out how to get their shit together, and I would have to close down my business and go back to selling forklifts because all y'all figured out the secret sauce recipe for getting organized.

Turns out time wasn't what was needed to get organized, but rather skill and heaps of motivation to get it done.

There is also another factor for which I have no better name for than "fed-upness," meaning you are so fed up with your situation you are going to do whatever it takes to fix it, short of burning it all to the ground and starting over. My guess is you've reached some level of fed-upness and interest, hence you've read this far into the book. Teaching you the skills needed with sprinkles of motivation is where I come in!

Another title for this book might have been *70 Percent Organized*, because when it comes to the applicable nature of being organized, the goal I want you to aim for is "passing." It's as simple as either failing or passing, and you only need a 70 to get that term credit. There is no honor roll for A-plus student organizers. If my academic history is any indication of my success, I was barely a B minus on my best days, and—news flash—the Dean's List of Most Organized does not exist. Social media has tricked you into believing it's a simple step-by-step process and *boom*: you've got an immaculate house. Remember that these influencers are using affiliate links to sell you stuff, and creating those organizing videos is their source of income, aka their job. No shade; I do the same! In fact, it's one of my biggest motivators to organize or even reorganize my own spaces—so I can record it and repurpose it into content.

Can we take a moment to normalize *stuff*? Let's not call

it clutter for a minute. Clutter seems to have evolved into a category of #allthethings that have no business existing, but my workout bag or shoes aren't in and of themselves clutter. Items cross the threshold into clutter when they are in the way—a tripping hazard for anyone walking in our tiny shared laundry/mud/utility room.

Here's a fun fact you didn't ask for: the etymology of the word "clutter" comes from the root of the word "clot" or "coagulate," as in stuff that piles up on top of each other. Perhaps keeping the stuff to a single layer is normal—for example, the suitcase on the floor from your most recent trip. But we cross the line from stuff to clutter when we collect several travel bags never fully unpacked from several different trips over the course of a frequent flyer vacation revenge summer—like my 2023 summer. This also applies to spaces in your home. You have the skincare routine you're currently using, but a new regimen caught your eye—so you purchased it, and now it's all sitting on your counter. It's stuff—now eating up every square inch of your bathroom (which, in full disclosure, is my current nightmare). As an acne sufferer since I was a young teen and now almost graduating from my thirties, I have gone through waves of buying everything that promises to clear my skin. In the agony of breakouts I'm pretty vulnerable, and that has led to overbuying skincare and therefore the excessive clutter in my bathroom. I have a feeling many women have been sold the promise of pretty by the beauty industry, bought more

than they needed, and then felt guilty about their overconsumption. This is clutter, the layers on top of layers of new regimens promising to give you glass skin—but absolutely clutter we can tackle together.

If you left your groceries on your counter and never put them away so they prevented you from using the counter—the groceries you purchased for the week become clutter. But *stuff* is normal and is allowed to exist in your home. It's important to draw the distinction between stuff—your kids' backpacks and current school papers—versus clutter, which is the heaps of unidentifiable objects piled, causing confusion and stress. Even in Mayan ruins they found dishes and *stuff*, and I'm pretty sure these ancient families occasionally fought over who had to clear the table. The point: for thousands of years, we as *Homo sapiens* have been acquiring and keeping items we need to use in our homes. All that *stuff* in your house was brought in with the intent of using it beneficially. When you no longer use it and the purpose is null or you're just ready for a change, then it's time to label that item as clutter and move it on out.

Many hesitate and are stuck in the "one day what if?" mindset. *Maybe* one day you'll finally do that furniture upcycle project. What if you *do need* that fourth extra cooler for a party? *Maybe* one day you'll learn how to crochet. What if you *do fit* into that size again? All these are valid considerations, but bear in mind that if you do keep that item, it will be clutter until you incorporate using it in your life. Given the ease and cheapness of acquiring *stuff*, I'd be willing to bet that if that day comes this year, next year, or in 10 years, you can purchase what is needed to use at that time. In the meantime, the space in your home and in your mind is more valuable than the possible future cost of acquiring the item again.

Getting your life organized is one of the most commonly made New Year's resolutions. We also see a surge in the goal of organizing during spring cleaning frenzy, when the snow melts in colder regions, and when kids go back to school in the fall after having taken over the house all summer long. It's time to apply practicality to this very common resolution of getting organized. Being organized makes our day-to-day lives easier to manage, and shouldn't that be the goal? What can we organize to make your life feel easier? That should be the root of your goal: organizing is the task that results in giving us freedom and more space in our lives.

We can keep pretending that the minimalist approach with everything stored in clear bins and sorted by color in ROYGBIV rainbow order is achievable in every space—but it's time we all recognize the truth. For the majority of us, a system like that is not maintainable. Those who seemingly have their ducks in a row actually hire help or have live-in nannies who help co-manage their household clutter. It could be one person's full-time job to maintain organizing systems in a household with three kids, two dogs, and a partridge in a pear tree. For the rest of us who manage busy households, maintain employment, raise wild kids, and have some sort of social life that doesn't include making YouTube cleaning videos—we can't keep juggling all the balls and expect to add "perfectly organized house" into the rotation. And so #sorrynotsorry—there, I said it.

I know what you're thinking: maybe *this* book will finally light the fire under my ass and get my life in order? Cue sigh of exhaustion. It is my hope that this book hits a little differently than most organizing books. While I too swoon over the pages full of glamorous homes with rainbow-ordered everything, I find these standards insanely difficult to reach and maintain. Then, if you're adding on any neurodivergent spice such as attention-deficit/hyperactivity disorder (ADHD) or obsessive-compulsive disorder (OCD), you may find yourself in an unsustainable vortex of expectations. When you deal with a neuro-spicy quality, or multiple like myself, doing and completing any task requires mental gymnastics with a flawless stick landing, particularly an organizing project in your home. It's important to recognize these obstacles, have patience with yourself, and slowly make changes toward a more organized life.

My hope is that this book meets you where you are, acknowledging the chapter of life you are in as well as any special qualities about you that you endure. We leave the comparison monster behind and decide to just be more organized than we were yesterday. The only one in the race is you.

Chapter 1

WHO THE HECK AM I?

Hey there! I'm Meggie, owner of Organized Life Design and badass organizing extraordinaire. We have been serving clients in Houston, Texas, and the surrounding Gulf Coast for the last decade—yes, that's before the Netflix organizing shows were a thing. (Actually that's back when Netflix mailed you a DVD—yes, like stamped postage via USPS—one or two movies at a time, putting Blockbuster out of business. If you were born after 2000 you'll have to look that up on your own; we don't have that kind of time here.) Being a professional organizer was a dream planted in my heart and mind during my teens. I have been organizing for hundreds of clients over the last 10 years in every type of space imaginable—from playrooms to pantries and hair salons to closets full of more shoes than you could wear in one year, changing your footwear daily.

Fast-forward to my life today. I'm a mama to two smart and sassy girls, married to a loud-mouthed Italian, and trying to keep from doing a reenactment of SpongeBob running around town screaming. I'm a dog mom to two dirt-loving creatures who enjoy tearing up as much trash as they can find. Like many of you, all these hats I wear pull my life in different directions and make it all the more challenging to keep up with the house.

Sometimes I wish my brain weren't so meticulous. It feeds a constant anxiety that makes relaxing hard for me. Every space I walk into starts my neurotransmitters firing—looking for ways to sort, order, and perfect. I simply can't turn it off, which means I deal with this affliction in every space of my own home even when I truly don't want to care. I'm still amazed that I was able to turn this natural skill into a paying profession, even if it can be exhausting at times. I'm looking forward to sharing these skills with you later in the book—once we establish this as the right time for you to design your organized life.

yogurt
sides
sweets
chocolate
spindrift
HOLY KOMBUCHA
eggs
eggs
eat me
bread
ClimateZone
fruit
veggies
MILD CHEDDAR
cheese
deli

READY FOR A NEW MINDSET?

Being organized is a state of being, much like being healthy. Contrary to popular belief, how organized you are is not measured by looks. It also applies to how healthy someone is, and a person's outward appearance is not always a reflection of their overall health and wellness. If I'm in good shape, it means I'm focused on my well-being, snacking smart, and finding time to work out three to four times a week. The true measure of my health is how I feel about my energy level and sleep quality, not whether light can pass through my thighs while standing in a bathing suit (it cannot and hasn't since I hit puberty at age 10). Health is an internal state of mind. Attempts at reaching a health goal can be as frustrating as attempts to become organized. So if you have experienced letdowns in the past—health and organization alike—don't be discouraged, my friend. These processes and journeys are what bring flavor to life. You're not alone in this adventure, and we'll laugh and cry along the way together!

The most successful people living healthy lifestyles will tell you it requires a mindset shift—one that didn't happen overnight like flipping a light switch, but rather a slow shift over time and most assuredly with mistakes along the way. They have formed a collective group of habits including water consumption, getting seven to eight hours of sleep every night, eating balanced meals, and breaking a sweat a few times a week, leading to feeling healthier and more energetic. Note I said that in a way as though it were an improvement in status rather than an extreme example from completely out of shape to weightlifting model. We all know that "results not typical" warning label on every fitness program the algorithm shoves down your throat. This same warning could be added to perfectly styled organized interiors. We want to aim for more organized and less stressed about clutter.

This is the way I want you to approach the goal of being organized—it's a way of living. It asks you to bring less into the home, manage your belongings well, and carve out time each week to reset systems. I want you to be ruthless about what comes into your home. Treat potential clutter like a solicitor trying to sell you a service at your front door. Sometimes you should ignore the doorbell! Think long and hard if it sounds like something you really need—and most of the time the answer should be "No, thanks."

Identifying a pivotal point that marks this shift in your life can be powerful. Many who choose to embrace a healthy way of life often do so based on a life-altering event—perhaps losing a loved one to illness or facing their own health scare—which is traumatic enough to ignite the change. The resulting mindset shift keeps them motivated to stay the course with their new lifestyle long past any fad. Let the meltdown you had last weekend about the piles of stuff making you feel chaotic and confused be the pivotal moment. If there's no outburst to note, create positive motivation: plan a big birthday bash at your house in three months to light the fire under your ass and put your organizing into high gear.

This is the moment you've decided to make a shift. It doesn't mean that everything is smooth sailing from here. Even those undertaking major weight loss journeys have weight fluctuations; some weeks you will plateau or even go backward. What keeps you going is the "why" behind your goal. Think about the reason you want to live an organized life. What is your "why"? Really dig deep. I mean, who actually gives a fuck about your house? Honestly. Are you trying to impress the mom group when it's your turn to host a playdate? That is a futile motivator, because the superficial "I don't want people to judge me" bit isn't enough. Are you hoping to show off in TikTok videos about how amazing your life is? A great way to feel empty is basing your approval on the clicks of strangers.

For many of our clients, the pursuit of becoming more organized comes from the desire to feel freedom and to enjoy their lives more. Clutter should never hold us back from doing amazing things and living our best lives even if that's having one day a week to truly relax. The burden of clutter is too trivial and unimportant to be the deterrent that keeps us from enjoying our families and making time for adventures.

Here is where the test of pass or fail comes into play. Are the piles of laundry and other stuff keeping you from the life you want to live? Pass or fail? Does being disorganized prevent you from achieving your health goals or earning a degree or dating again or advancing in your career? If the answer is no, then congrats, queen! You are gettin' it!

On the other hand, if your life feels held back by a lack of organizing systems in your home, then I got you, boo.

ABOUT ME AND MY WHY

I am truly obsessed with organizing. If organizing were a '90s boy band, I would be the gosh darn president of the fan club. I have been the nerd engaged with systems and functionality since I was a kid. It started in the checkout lanes of the grocery store in my preschool years. While most kids were asking their mommies if they could buy Skittles or a Snickers bar, I was the cute little geek with rad fringe bangs straightening up the candy aisle—putting the Kit Kats with Kit Kats and fluffing the M&M's bags. Candy needed to be sorted, straightened, and ready for purchase. You're welcome for all the free labor, Kroger. As a preteen, no one ever had to ask me to clean my room. I thrived and focused best on schoolwork when my space was neat and tidy. Keeping things organized was built into my DNA.

As a super cool 14-year-old who was not on any sports teams and not popular by any standard, I had a pretty open social calendar. This provided the space in my schedule to help a friend's mom tackle organizing her house. My friend's parents had gone through a difficult divorce, which had been particularly stressful for his mom. During the separation, the clutter had accumulated in piles throughout her home, and I was there as the extra hands to help her go through it room by room. She paid with a couple of twenties and free meals to comb through the piles that had accumulated during the demise of her marriage. Depression and heartbreak had consumed her energy, and her house reflected her pain. Little by little we made our way through the stacks and piles. From the family room and living room to the kitchen and her bedroom, every space needed attention. I could see how the clutter had clouded an already traumatic situation and was affecting her ability to heal her mental health. Experiencing how our space can impact our spirit became a core memory for me.

I credit her as the one who took me on my first trip to The Container Store. Walking in felt as though the mothership had called me home. I was in awe. Angels sang as the doors opened to this magical place filled with bins and baskets and order and efficiency. My friend's mom mentioned to the salesclerk that I was helping her organize, and the clerk responded with, "Oh, how great! You could be a professional organizer!"

"Excuse me, whaaa? Wait, hold the phone, *this* is a real job?! You mean, I can convert my internal OCD into something people will pay me for? Where do I sign up?" My mind exploded with the possibilities. I was so motivated to exercise my newly minted professional skill that

I completely reorganized my room and designed my own bookshelf system to hold my very on-trend-in-the-'90s 13-inch TV/VCR combo along with my VHS and CD collection. I designated another part of my room to be a mini desk area, outfitted with organizing goodies from my new headquarters, The Container Store.

This experience planted the seed. As we worked through the spaces in my friend's mom's home and the clutter began to diminish, I watched her become less stressed. She seemed to find bits of hope and purpose again. Her demeanor seemed lighter and less strained, and she was freed from the burden hidden in the piles. From my point of view, she felt she had a better handle on her home and, therefore, a better outlook on her life—something I would come to understand even more personally when I went through a divorce ten years later.

For me, it was the perfect testament to the power of creating a serene space and the positive impact it can have on your psyche. Taking control of your space is an extension of taking control of your life—or at least the part on which you have the most influence. We have almost zero influence on the actions and behaviors of our family, friends, and coworkers, but in our personal space and attitude, we can effect change. It was the moment I knew this was what I wanted to do with my life: I wanted to make this sort of positive impact on as many people's lives as I possibly could.

Just for
Princesses

NO, I'M NOT A MINIMALIST

In my college years, I owned about 25 articles of clothing and six dishes, so you bet I could easily keep my apartment in tip-top shape. Also note that my roommate was even neater than I was and my only dependent was a cat. My social life consisted of fewer parties than I have toes during the entirety of my four-year college residence (**cough** DORK! **cough**).

I know what you're thinking: this girl must have been on the dean's list! You'd be wrong again. Actually, I was a B-average student with two jobs. My hours were filled as a student, a bank teller, and a piano teacher. I wanted to graduate with as little student debt as possible, so I worked as much as I could to pay my living expenses. While my college lifestyle may sound like a ringing endorsement for minimalism, that's not exactly what I'm advocating (but no shade if that's your jam!).

There is no denying the fact that the more you own, the more time is required to manage what you own. The less you have to manage in your space, the less time it will take you to manage those items. Knowing this truth should influence a thicker filter for what you want to bring into your home. Minimalism can also make it easier to avoid clutter and escape the sense of being overwhelmed by your stuff. I get it; I do. I understand the appeal, and the simplicity has its own vibe. But minimalism is not a church I have decided to join. I'm one of those people who likes to vacation somewhere new every time I buy a plane ticket, and I rarely order the same thing off a menu. I have a love for fashion and a thing for books, the kind you hunt for in a used bookstore. Add kids and their interests and hobbies in the mix and I simply can't comprehend how to be a minimalist. My daughters seem to have been born with an affinity for maximalism, and not only do they want to keep everything but they also want to acquire as much as possible. They are tiny little collectors of everything from rocks to Barbies to every page they have ever colored.

Life was much simpler when it was just my cat and me back in college. It was easier to manage and easier to stay organized. Fast-forward to my life after college—I got married, we bought a house, I began nesting, and then we got divorced. That's a story for another book, so we'll skip ahead once more.

Then I got married again, and we had two ridiculously gorgeous and intelligent daughters.

Want to know the cleanest my house has ever been since having kids almost a decade ago? My current husband and I went through a tumultuous time in our marriage and separated. (Also a story for another book.) He moved into an apartment with most of his stuff about a mile from our home to make co-parenting as easy as possible. We alternated weeks with our girls: they would stay with me one week and with him the next. It seemed to make sense to swap on the weekends and keep school days and activities as streamlined as possible.

The void I felt when they left after my week of parenting was almost unbearable. In an effort to combat my sadness and loneliness, I cleaned and organized my house whenever I wasn't at work or the gym. In every room, I deep-cleaned and reorganized systems that were already organized. My house was as pristine as it had ever been and as empty as it had ever felt. There were times I sat on my couch and couldn't think of anything else to clean or another project to complete.

We often think we'll find more happiness if our homes are in perfect order and all the projects are done—but I'm here to tell you, you'd miss the mess. I promise you would invite the chaos back because of the loved ones who come with it. You would miss your husband's gym bag on the floor of the mudroom, the toys in the living room, the blanket forts in the bedroom, and the dirty dishes from a full table of dinner guests. Creating these memories comes with making a bit of a mess. Let's find a way to appreciate the mess of making memories, too.

FINDING THE BALANCE

There is certainly a threshold for clutter that gives you the freedom to create memories without losing sight of what truly matters. Seek the balance between a passing level of organization and enjoying the life you have created. I've heard so many clients and followers blame their kids and their spouse as the biggest culprit of clutter, and you know what—they're absolutely right. If you didn't have a messy spouse leaving a trail in every room or your precious little chaos gremlins, also known as your offspring, tearing through your house like tiny tornadoes, then yes, your house could be immaculate. Yet in my personal experience, the absence of clutter doesn't equal bliss.

Perhaps the clutter surrounding you isn't anyone's but your own—remember true contentedness is found within. There is a lightness you will find in cleaning up your space, but the true fun begins when you are able to host dinner with friends because you are no longer embarrassed to have people into your home. You will feel freer not because you have less stuff, but the weight of stuff is lifted from your spirit. The clutter isn't stopping you from being able to pursue bigger dreams outside of four walls. The satisfaction isn't only about getting organized, but also about the next chapter, in which opportunities open around you.

I'M A FREAKING PROFESSIONAL!

Let's jump to the present. I'm a busy small business owner with even busier kids, trying my best to hold it all together with prayer and superglue. I have all the systems in place to help me be organized. I'm a freaking professional! Yet I still struggle to keep clutter at bay everywhere in my house. In fact, as I write this book, I want to slam my laptop closed because I

Jenga
crafty fashion show
Don't Break the Ice
Let's Go Fishin'
Deluxe Edition
Zingo!
Zingo!
Cootie
CHESS · CHECKERS
CHINESE CHECKERS
SUPERHEROES
DIG IT UP!
SUPER-FUN
MARBLE RUN
Monkey Around
Hungry Hungry Hippos
Puppy Puffle
MANCALA
OPERATION
I SPY preschool Game
SCRABBLE
Phonics Stamps
WHEATIES
MONOPOLY
SORRY!
SORRY!
Rummikub
THE ALLOWANCE GAME
Best Friends
TEA PARTY
CANDY LAND

feel like a fraud. How could I possibly write a book on getting organized when I have several laundry mountains in my house and unpacked boxes in my entryway? And the truth is, this isn't a book about getting organized with 50 beautiful photos of rainbow-sorted goodness. No hate, but to me, all that stuff is as good as a smutty book. This is a book about changing our attitude toward clutter, releasing ourselves from the shame and guilt it brings, and learning to make small adjustments to improve our quality of life until we have the funds, time, and energy to attack it all.

LET'S NORMALIZE CLUTTER

I want to normalize clutter—the exact opposite of the seemingly perfect influencer peddling some other Amazon trinket that I promise you don't need. When I say let's normalize clutter, I'm not referring to a person who keeps everything they have ever bought in a home that is bursting at the seams. There is a diagnosable condition known as "chronic disorganization" that is affiliated with ADHD and OCD, and in its most extreme form is referred to as hoarding. Thanks to a long-running reality TV show, most of us have a clear image of what that looks like in its most extreme, untreated state.

Normalizing clutter means harnessing the ability to untether ourselves and understand that living life to its fullest involves periods of mess. You are not weird or bad or abnormal because you're in a constant state of needing to do laundry. Not having to deal with laundry means you either live in a nudist colony or have exceptional wealth to afford someone else to take care of it, but it doesn't mean there is something wrong with you. Honestly, I have truly considered becoming a nudist for the appeal of zero laundry, but it seems impractical for activities like working out and cooking.

Once upon a time when I had a full-time job and pre-kids and pre-spouse, the only way I could snap my apartment back into its organized shape was to use designated vacation days and spend them putting all my shit back where it needed to go. Why? During the week, I was fitting in marathon training runs, trivia nights, and social gatherings on top of a full-time work schedule and a side hustle. The result of this packed life was clothes piled up, toiletries strewn on the bathroom counter, and mail left unopened.

Clutter accumulates as life unfolds. This. Is. Normal.

Even though I am a professional organizer and a member of the National Association of Productivity and Organizing Professionals since 2014, I am not exempt from acquiring clutter in my home. I used to feel like an imposter because the busier I became with helping clients get organized, the harder it was to manage my own household. Not to mention the tiny tornadoes and giant hurricane I live with who love to dump their crap on any and every surface. The four of us could create the perfect storm of chaos. My social media feeds were littered with a highlight reel of perfectly organized spaces in other homes, and I fell victim to the same comparison monster we all face: Why doesn't my house look like *that*?!

Why wasn't I giving myself the same grace I ask my clients to give themselves for not keeping my home together? Of course, I have to remind myself that those Instagrammers and YouTubers who produce those satisfying cleaning and restocking videos are also not working for other clients—and if they are, the space they are filming isn't likely their own.

Did you know that fashion influencers often have two closets—one they film from and pose in outfits in, which they refer to as their office, and one they actually use with their normal real clothes that can't be tagged with affiliate links? I want more "Instagram vs. reality" reels from home lifestyle accounts that are overflowing with DIY and organizing videos. More of their perfect in-the-moment spaces while the rest of the room holds their clutter just out of the viewing frame (in case you were wondering how I present myself on social media). If you don't follow me yet, come join the party, amiga! It's important to me to keep it real online, so yes, I brag about our work with clients, but I mostly share my own spaces and challenges and focus on helping teach you the skills you need to design a more organized life.

Does every chef cook their own three-course dinner every night? No. What about the nutritionist who eats ice cream every weekend? So what. In the early years of my company, I felt like I had to portray myself as a perfect homemaker. It's hard to make this DGAF (don't give a fuck), tattoo-laden, purple-hair-wearin' *chingona* (badass) blush—but boy, would I, when a neighbor caught a glimpse of my unkempt garage. My clutter was a dirty little secret, because why would anyone hire me if I had any clutter in my house?

But let me be the first to tell you, that shit was exhausting! Then I was introduced to Brené Brown, the queen of vulnerability, via her HBO special. She has written book after book on the power of being vulnerable and how it makes us better leaders, better parents, and better friends. She has given TED Talks on the impact vulnerability has on relationships. In this particular special she admitted that her knowledge of the subject of vulnerability is definitely a grade A, but admitted she might only earn a C plus in the practice of the very subject that is synonymous to her research. Holy cheese and rice! What a freaking lightbulb moment for me. It was amazing to hear her honest admission and ironically how fucking *vulnerable* of her to admit she didn't feel like she was perfect at the practice of being vulnerable.

I AM YOU!

I'm embracing vulnerability. It is the reason I'm different from a lot of those you find on the "For You" pages you receive all the time on social media. I have given the façade the middle finger! I'm done pretending I don't struggle keeping my house together while being a full-time working mom with two active kids. In fact, I realized it was exactly what was hindering me from connecting with you. The truth is, I AM YOU! That's right, I struggle to ignore the same Instagram ads for things I don't need—yet the promise of being sexier, smarter, and happier sounds so alluring, I click "add to cart" anyway.

The only teeny tiny difference is that my hyperfocus mentality eventually kicks into overdrive and I'm able to channel it into a project in my home. My OCD, along with help from buckets of the legal stimulant coffee, conjoins to see an organized project to completion out of sheer stubbornness. That is, of course, as long as I'm not overexhausted from 30-plus hours of on-site organizing for clients or the 20-plus hours of administrative paperwork and emails always waiting for me.

The largest motivation for maintaining my own abode is the fact that I do this for a living, and every project takes on a dual function as content and advertising for my company. Organizing and reorganizing my own spaces give me a chance to refine my skills or try new organizing products or labeling systems before they are introduced to a client's space.

I feel this organizing book is different from many of those you may have read. And by read, I mean purchased, perused the first six pages, and then watched it collect dust on your bookshelf for the next five years. This one is different. First, I want us to be friends—like the kind of amigas who are completely themselves around each other, no filters. It also means I'll let the cuss words fly and I won't hold back when tough love is needed. Second, I'm hilarious.

This is not your average self-help book full of eye-numbing, bored-stiff repetitive drool. It's a humorous, easy-to-read book like those you keep on the back of your toilet for guests—though I do question why you even want your guests to shit in your house in the first place; no need to make them that comfortable. Third, we're in this journey together. We know this is a marathon and not a sprint, but babe, this is not a race you have to run alone.

As with a health journey, your organizing journey is a muscle that needs tending. You need to do things to strengthen your muscles and keep them strong, and the same is true for your organizing and system-keeping skills. There are times you pull a muscle and need to listen to your body and take a break. The same holds true if this organizing adventure becomes overwhelming: listen to your mind and take a break.

You will need to tweak things along the way, and as life and interests change, spaces will need to be adjusted. There will be seasons when organizing is easier to manage and other times when you want to light a match and start all over from scratch because the challenge in front of you feels impossible. For legal reasons, I must encourage you not to do so, as I do not recommend starting fires as an organizing technique. It may seem appealing and effective, I understand—believe me, *I understand*—but the aftermath is not worth the jail time. I will never have a perfect house; you will never have a perfect house. Remember, perfection isn't the goal—a passing grade is. While we're at it, let's also shift our attitude about clutter and find a balance that feels better in our bodies and allows us more peace of mind.

Chapter 2

WHY SHOULD I CARE ABOUT CLUTTER?

SHIFTING ATTITUDES

First, I want us to pause; take a long, deep breath; and forgive ourselves for wherever we are. It's too easy to blame ourselves for overconsumption or falling short of homemaker duties. The worst—the statement I hear most often from clients, the one that makes me cringe—is when individuals call themselves lazy. My dear, sweet friend, you are NOT lazy—but you ARE muthafucking exhausted. I see

you. I see all the things you are doing. I see everything you are trying to be for everyone else. You are depleted, and the last thing you have time to care about is how organized your garage is right now. You have lost any remaining fucks you had and have none to spare for your closet, the playroom, or the pantry. In those moments of torture when you're "should-ing" all over yourself about how organized you should be, remember that even God rested on the seventh day. That's right, the Almighty Creator of the universe took a day off—which means you have to learn to give yourself rest too. I relate to the internal battle of giving ourselves a needed dose of grace. I've said many times to clients that the only person to die with a finished to-do list was Jesus, and that dude had 12 assistants. Be kinder to yourself.

There is a lot of self-appointed, unsubstantiated shame and guilt we hold in regard to the clutter in our homes. We incorrectly associate shame and guilt with the clutter we have accumulated in our lives. Why? It's a result of the money we spent racking up credit card bills and the space the stuff consumes in our homes and the time sucked up in managing it all. All these factors play a role in our emotions about clutter. Babe, let's cut ourselves some slack. Not only is it easier than ever before to consume (excuse me, rhymes with Glamazon Slime), but it's also far cheaper. There are entire stores dedicated to selling shit for a dollar or for less than five dollars, so we end up buying a LOT of it without considering the aftermath.

YOU, my friend, are not a unique consumer. The constant advertising for us to buy more stuff is at every corner on everything we watch, everything we hear, and everything we see. The little device we keep in our hand 99 percent of the time is designed to keep us buying and consuming. It's listening to you, learning what you like, what your pain points are, your favorite sports team—it even knows if you're moving. I'm convinced the algorithm knows me better than my spouse or mother sometimes, considering the purchase ideas continually suggested to me.

You are not the only one duped by these ads and marketing tactics. All of us are. We don't even have to leave our houses anymore to consume in the way most of us did before the turn of the century. Anything on the global marketplace is available for purchase at any hour of the day and can arrive at your doorstep without you even having to put on pants. Think about the huge difference that is from what was available to us in the past. Consider what the intricacies of buying a book used to be: you had to get in your car, drive along roads through traffic, pay for your book, and bring it home. Today, with the tap of one finger, that book will show up on your doorstep tomorrow . . . along with a million other items, if you want them.

The cost of consuming is also less, although it doesn't feel that way in this era of inflation. There weren't big-box stores 50 years ago stocked with bulk items or a supercenter of crap on every corner of every city. No wonder so many of us have houses bursting at the seams. Newsflash, it is actually MOST of us! There's a reason professional organizing is one of the fastest-growing industries in the past decade and continues to grow year over year. Again, YOU are just like so many of your friends and neighbors—those you think have perfectly kept homes from your peek into their front windows—but remember, all their clutter is simply hiding in their closets and cabinets and drawers.

CONSUMING WITH SCRUTINY

We can't get hung up on the money we've spent or the space the stuff we've bought consumes. That's about as useful as dwelling upon the person you went on three dates with almost a decade ago and wondering why it fizzled out. It doesn't freaking matter! The past is done. That chapter is over. The shit is already here. Rather than beating ourselves up about how it got here, let's make a pact to do better starting right now. No more self-berating sessions—only looking forward. That means consuming with scrutiny. It requires running past the dollar spot at Target like your cart is on fire. It means finally coming to terms with the seven pairs of pants two sizes too small that we keep thinking what if, maybe someday—and instead facing the beautiful reality of our changing, aging bodies. If by some miracle potato chips stop tasting delicious or you jump on the GLP-1 train and could actually fit that size again, I want you to budget for new pants. Pretty sure potato chips are gonna hold the line, so it is time to break up with those suckers.

Now then, we've established it's easier to consume clutter than it is to make toast.

Can we all forgive ourselves for being in the position in which we find ourselves? The groundless shame and guilt will hold us hostage in this place and may even perpetuate the cycle of consumption. I pray you are able to move past those unproductive feelings of guilt and shame that do nothing to motivate our spirits but actually hold us back from stepping into the future.

Can we please give that wasted sack of shame the middle finger? Buh-bye! Suck a bag of dicks, guilt!

We have to learn from our situation, but we can't let it take over our hearts and minds. It's important to keep our motivation in mind so we make better choices in the future. Will you be perfect? No. Do you now want to try and make better decisions about consumption that fit your new more peaceful, easier-to-manage life? I hope so. Letting shame and guilt overtake us will not get us to the other side of this mess. Enough is enough.

Guilt and shame, be gone. Fuck off.

WHY CARE?

Why do we even care if we are organized? As we discussed in the beginning, the goal is to be organized enough to keep clutter from holding us back from the life we want to be living. It is about creating just enough space to feel gaps of freedom and peace in our homes. The obsession with consuming and managing stuff cannot be the hurdle that stops you from being the person you were meant to be. Let's examine why it's such an important goal and one of the top New Year's resolutions year after year.

Clutter truly does hinder our ability to achieve progress. It distracts us from enjoying our lives and living more freely. Clutter takes our attention away from our spouses, our kids, and our loved ones. It's what I call physical noise, constantly calling for our attention.

"Hey, Jennifer. Here I am! It's me, the stack of mail that's been growing exponentially on your kitchen counter for three months. Hey, Jenn, look at me multiply."

"Hey, Lauren, remember me? I'm the room of unfinished crafts you started but didn't have the skills, time, or patience to finish. I am just sitting here rotting and bringing you dread. Remember all that money you spent on me at Michaels?"

Clutter demands our time and our energy. Hell, clutter is one reason it's taken me so long to write this book. I literally had to leave my house and the city where I live to find enough space and distance to focus on writing large parts of this book. No matter what I do, if I'm home, I find myself folding laundry or doing dishes like it's a never-ending prison sentence. Sometimes when I'm home you'll find me paralyzed on the couch watching *Bridgerton*, but that's a conversation for later when I address my experiences with mental health and the role it plays in clutter and disorganization. The fact is we have to address that FIRST and foremost before we are able to go on this journey.

Now—back to how distracting clutter can be.

I too feel the tinge of guilt if I'm leaving the house for some fun prescheduled activity when there's a round of shipping boxes in my entryway taller than my seven-year-old. Should I really be heading to this event, or should I be addressing the mountain of clutter in my bedroom? One of the most obvious ways one experiences clutter as a distraction is when you're trying to work from home. It's extremely difficult to focus on emails and clients when there's a dining room of mayhem staring you down the entire time. You're talking through project management or trying to secure a new client, but the clutter in the corner never shuts the hell up.

WTF IS ALL THIS SHIT?

For years, my parents assumed the clients I worked for were all hoarders, based on the premise of the popular TV show of the same name, which featured homes overrun with actual garbage, even leading to issues with rodents. These people were often on the verge of eviction based on the dilapidated state of their houses; sometimes they were so far under the figurative water of their clutter that the city they lived in was threatening to condemn their properties based on the

DINOBLOCK
PRIDE & PREJUDICE
Tillman
Dinner at the Panda Palace
COLORS

hazard they posed to their communities. Interestingly, these individuals were often not the ones reaching out for help but rather the ones being voluntold by a family member who had run out of options for dealing with the clutter and lacked the resources to change the situation. On the show, a licensed professional was always overseeing the project and constantly checking in with the homeowner.

Deep-rooted trauma and depression can manifest in an unmanageable home environment. These hoarders were dealing with so much pain that it took over their lives and their spaces.

Let's get one thing straight: being a hoarder is a diagnosable condition. In recent years, hoarding has been diagnosed as a chronic disorganized disorder or chronic disorganization that often parallels and accompanies ADD, ADHD, depression, anxiety disorders, and more.[1] This psychological challenge involves deep-rooted fears of scarcity that are best discussed with a mental health professional before the task of decluttering even comes into the picture. Being a disorganized hot mess leading to stress, which leads to paralysis about how to tackle our disorganized hot mess is more a rampant first-world overconsumption

---

1 Phyllis Flood Knerr, "Factors Associated with Disorganization," Institute for Challenging Disorganization, accessed April 16, 2025, https://www.challengingdisorganization.org/wp-content/uploads/2024/06/ICD-fs004-Factors-Associated-with-Disorganization-2024.pdf.

virus that is spreading faster than COVID. Babe, I've been diagnosed at least three times with both of those problems! Being deemed a hoarder is not the same thing as simply being disorganized. I do, however, believe we can have hoarding tendencies. Hoarding is keeping things that no longer hold value to you . . . in excess.

In my experience, I do see more hoarding tendencies with older generations, in particular among those who survived the Great Depression, like my adopted GG (short for great-grandmother). Similar to the worry we experienced during the pandemic regarding our toilet paper supply or the inability to get our favorite gluten-free bread, these individuals actually experienced food and other commodity shortages that have led to an aversion to discarding.

Our greatest generation and the generation that followed, the silent generation, had to be scrappy and resourceful. Everything had value during the Great Depression years. I understand how this kind of trauma was ingrained in their thought processes, especially those who experienced it during their tender years of growth. They feel everything can be reused or repurposed, even the plastic takeout container from the local Asian restaurant. They have a constant fear of scarcity looming and feel they cannot get rid of anything that may be useful. From canned foods to paper scraps, these survivors have a predilection for all things no matter the last time they may have used them and in spite of actual plans to use them anytime in the future. My GG would keep those plastic containers you buy store-bought muffins in, wash them, and hold onto them with plans of reusing them. I do not judge but rather use this knowledge to gauge a greater understanding when working for these clients. I always encourage them to make the hard choices while focused on the goal of the changes that will make their lives easier and help them find more freedom.

As I said before and bears repeating: the more stuff we own, the more time it takes to manage the stuff. The less stuff we own, the less time needed to manage it, which opens up more time for all the other activities and interests we want to enjoy. Here are some questions I challenge clients to ponder but we would all do well to ask ourselves:

- What happens if I get rid of this [insert useful object here]?
- Will it be very costly to purchase again later?
- Will it be difficult to locate later?
- Where do I store it if I keep it?
- Is the space needed to store it taking up room I could use for something else more valuable or important?

There is always a cost associated with keeping the object, as well as the time required to manage it and the space it takes up in your home. There is also a cost that comes with donating or discarding an object that may—perhaps, possibly—one day need to be acquired again. Essentially, the question to ask is: Can I buy it again if needed in the future without selling my kidney on the black market? If the answer is yes, it sounds like it can go for now. The cost of your time is something harder to quantify, but I'd calculate it to be something in the range of priceless.

Often clients think they are hoarding when truly they're just sentimental, and there is nothing wrong with that. Keeping items that hold special memories is part of who we are as humans. Should you keep every single outfit your children wore after you've closed the door on more kids? Instead, try keeping a few favorites and donate the rest to a worthy family. Do we hold on to every camera photo you had developed in the '80s and '90s? You might consider filling an album and ditching the ones with unidentifiable faces or blurry trees.

My youngest at the time of this writing is six and about to graduate from kindergarten. The toddler years were a blast of memories, but I'm super okay with fewer diapers and fewer tantrums. Yes, each stage of parenting has its unique set of challenges, but I am entering my best mom era in these elementary years. My daughter has given me her blessing to sell her play kitchen set, which has been sitting there stacked with all the plastic hot dogs and felt fruit. The cute pretend dishes and utensils are ready to go—yet I cannot do it. I walk past it constantly, which is in my way in our tight single hallway, and I can't bring myself to let it go. I can't count the number of pretend sandwiches I ate or play cups of tea I drank. I'm not ready yet, so the little retro-styled turquoise toy kitchen sits there until I can let it go.

Since we're getting nostalgic, I am the first to brag that I hit the jackpot with mothers-in-law. The nightmare stories we hear about husbands' mothers did not apply to mine. Heartbreakingly, my time with her was cut far too short six years ago when a car accident took her life. My spouse's dear mama was a woman who would hug you uncomfortably long, but with every ounce of love and compassion. She was the kind of person who wouldn't just RSVP to your party; she'd show up early and ask how she could help you get set up and stay long after to help you clean up. Her funeral was standing room only—so many people were touched by her spirit and infectious kindness.

These many years later, we miss her the same every day. Up until about six months ago we had two storage units full of her stuff. I wouldn't take anything away from the beautiful life she lived. These memories were painful and stressful and required a lot of emotional energy to go through. There is no rule as to how long you should take to go through a loved one's belongings after they have passed. I've had clients reach out for help months later and also decades later—only when the clutter had become a burden and they were finally ready to take a next step. This is where methods like Swedish death cleaning make sense. That method of decluttering is specifically tailored to purging so that what you leave behind doesn't burden the loved ones who remain.

If you are able, organizing your stuff now lessens the burden it may be on your loved ones down the road.

CLUTTER IS LOUD

The *Merriam-Webster Dictionary* defines clutter as "a crowded or confused mass or collection" or "things that clutter a place."[2] We all know what it is because we all have at least a little clutter in our lives, and most of us have a lot.

The real truth is clutter is visual noise, and cheese and rice, is it loud! Your clutter is screaming for your attention—deal with me. Put me away. Give me your attention. Just as a toddler is audible noise, a stack of papers sits on your desk like a hungry, tired kid whining loudly.

File, copy, send, research, pay, respond . . . the list of verbs to describe what has to be done with paper alone goes on and on. The mountains of unfolded and not-put-away laundry or the mound of toys your kids left out across the floor—always visually taking up space in your house and in your mind. When there are piles in every room, the volume can feel like you're at the club and the DJ is tuning it out—but instead of being at the club, that DJ is in your house and you're trying to be productive through the noise.

When we are surrounded by clutter, we are flooded with

---

2 "Clutter," *Merriam-Webster.com Dictionary*, Merriam-Webster, Accessed April 16, 2025. https://www.merriam-webster.com/dictionary/clutter.

emotions of stress, anxiety, depression, and overwhelm. Emotions can take over, and as a result, you are unable to live the life you want to be living and instead are paralyzed by the burden. You are not YOLO-ing or whatever fucking phrase is currently hip to the trick. (Clearly, I'm a millennial.) But in all transparency, your clutter is taking over your psyche—the visually screaming piles of clutter are bombarding your thoughts—and stopping you from pursuing your purpose here on this Earth.

WHAT THE HECK ARE YOU SUPPOSED TO DO?

Addressing the clutter can be overwhelming, especially when you face it alone. This is why the professional organizer industry is one of the fastest-growing industries of the last two decades.[3] From the books lining the bookshelves at Target to the reality shows streaming to the trendy line of products available and ready to ship to your home—our accumulation of stuff continues to grow, with accessibility easier, faster, and cheaper than it has ever been before.

I know that clearing the burden of clutter can be life-changing because I have seen it firsthand hundreds of times.

3 "Professional Organizing Industry Statistics & Future Outlook," Professional Organizer Mavericks, accessed June 5, 2024, https://professionalorganizermavericks.com/start/organizing-industry/.

It can be extraordinarily difficult to stick to a health plan if your pantry is a disaster and you can't keep your gym clothes clean. Starting a new career path can be daunting when the only place you have to study feels as if the walls are closing in and you can't find a working highlighter, even though you are sure you've bought at least two packs this month.

Clutter inhibits you from achieving goals, whether that's forging a new career path, achieving a health goal, or heck, even spending more quality time with your family playing games and eating dinner. We know life is already hard, no matter your story, and clutter is adding hurdles to leap over and hoops to jump through at every turn that will make it even more exhausting; it will sometimes even feel impossible.

That is why you're here—to give clutter the middle finger. It is time to put the distracting mess in its place.

Treat clutter like you should have treated that turd who made fun of you in middle school: fuck you, clutter.

IS THIS THE RIGHT TIME?

If you have a kid hanging off your tit, I'm gonna tell you right now and in all honesty, this would be a bad time to begin your organizing journey. I'm not hating on my new mamas; you are the superheroes. Perhaps you're two weeks into maternity leave and you're thinking, "Gosh, I have so much extra time because the baby sleeps so much. You know what I'll do? Get my house all organized!"

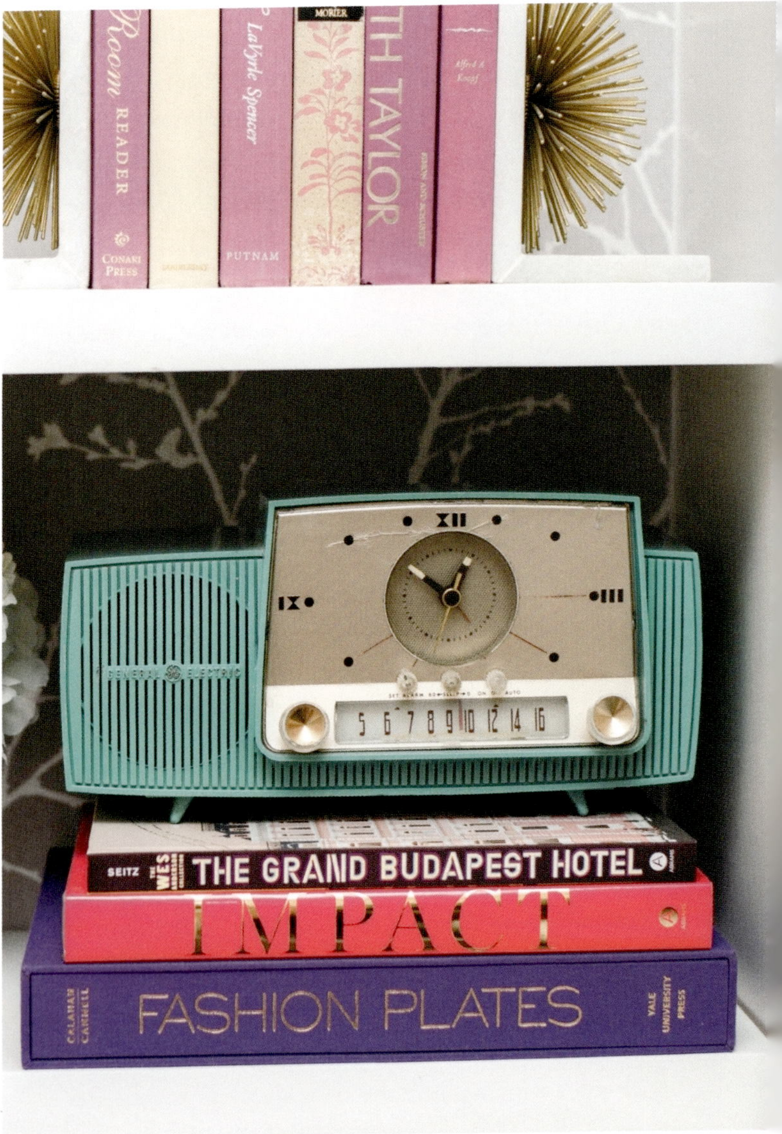

Room READER
CONARI PRESS
LaVyrle Spencer
PUTNAM
MORIER
TH TAYLOR
Alfred A. Knopf

Lemme stop you right there. Bless your darling heart with all those lofty goals, but my sweet, dear new mama, once the adrenaline of being a new mom wears off in the next 24 to 48 hours, you will be desperate to find 5 more minutes of sleep, so being in the middle of a pantry reorganization project would fall straight to the bottom of the priority list. Also worth adding here is how much your life will morph in the next few months as you establish new systems—it will be somewhat overwhelming as you see your life changing faster than you can keep up. Give yourself grace and save this book for a few months down the road.

It's important to also address those people who just started a new job or are wiping anyone else's ass besides their own, whether caring for children or aging relatives. I see you. You are in the middle of a lot right now and while I love you for buying this book, thanks for supporting this *Chicana*, but I ask that you please be kind to yourself if you start this book and it takes you months to finish it and even longer to organize one space. You already earned a gold star for being a supporter of a Hispanic woman-owned small business with your purchase. Yay for you! Let's be sure to set realistic expectations when it comes to your organizing goals so that we can make sure you are building confidence in your journey and not tearing yourself down because you can't do it all.

If this beach read you have here only makes you hire a professional organizing team because actually doing all these things is absolutely bananas, then I'm not mad about that, either. I'm proud of you for admitting you need help and reaching out, and again, being a small business advocate by hiring a local professional organizer. There's no shame for buying any DIY book and then not actually doing the DIY thing. No one is writing you a FAIL ticket for not completing the task you were intent on doing all by yourself. If that were the case, here are the following DIY intentions I would have FAIL tickets for: upholstering furniture, being an expert on the Gilded Age, sanding and staining wood furniture, repairing vintage record players, basically every type of cooking, learning how to crochet, starting a coffee shop, and many more bright ideas I no longer have aspirations of accomplishing.

The goal here was to create a readable-in-one-afternoon kind of book, because unless it's *Harry Potter* we don't need an intensely long novel to get this organizing thing done. I would be doing you a disservice if I didn't help you dig a little deeper before jumping ahead to the instructions. It's not my intention to present like one of those recipe blogs with 1,000 words on how the recipe originated out of mom's kitchen when all you want is gluten-free peanut butter cookies. However, from experience, in order to create a long-lasting shift, we first need to appreciate the benefits of adjusting our attitudes about clutter and give ourselves some grace. *Then* we can get a game plan for making our lives a little easier. At the end of the day, isn't that our true goal? To make our lives a little bit easier to manage? That there is the secret sauce.

At my company, Organized Life Design, our internal motto is "We do what we can to make our clients' lives easier," and that is what I want your goal to be for your organized life journey. Do what you can to make your life a little bit easier to manage. It is not about a grand gesture or every corner in your home being worthy of a *Martha Stewart Living* spread. If the only thing you establish is a consistent place for your car keys and you spend far less time searching for lost ones—bravo for you! I applaud you for making your life just a little bit easier to manage than it was previously.

So what is really stopping you from designing and living an organized life? It's you! Well, it's you and everyone who lives with you. We are our own worst enemy. This is where we do acknowledge our personal responsibility in the equation—sans shame and guilt—but also the time for what we Southerners call a "come-to-Jesus" moment with everyone who lives with you. You want to coordinate efforts with all parties responsible for the mess by asking for their buy-in. Getting the buy-in from those you live with is extremely effective for success in maintaining an organized home for the long haul and preventing as many future relapses as possible. Note I didn't say there would be zero. There is no chance in Hades you can maintain an organized home if you're the only one who cares that it is organized in the first place.

If you happen to be a mama with a spouse and three kids, guess what? You CANNOT do it all alone. Let me repeat, you CANNOT do it all. I know this is a tough pill to swallow. We are led to believe we can do it all, but unless you have a magic wand, then I regretfully must inform you this is neither achievable nor maintainable on your own without support from your family. As a side note, did you notice none of the households in the *Harry Potter* books or movies were perfectly clean and organized? Keep that in mind: even in the magical world, witches and wizards with actual magic wands couldn't maintain a perfectly arranged homestead.

Depending on the age of your offspring—or if it's just you and a roommate, spouse, or parent—a family meeting is recommended. You may be met with groans and eye-rolling, but keep the goal and motivation clear: "We want to clean up our home so that we can have more fun together. More organization, less fighting. More clutter accountability, less screaming in the mornings trying to get ready for school."

Remember, asking for the buy-in doesn't mean you get to dictate orders and everyone just has to follow suit. You have to be accountable too—which means before you holler about everyone leaving their shoes all over the place, don't forget to check the location of your own shoes first. This is something I am guilty of on a weekly basis. Changing attitudes doesn't happen overnight—it's a process of transition. Steps of progress in the right direction and increased family accountability is something to celebrate.

The point of this first household gathering is to establish

the goal of getting more organized, staying open to feedback and suggestions.

MENTAL HEALTH AND CLUTTER

There's a deep tie between the role of mental health and the relationship with clutter. Depression and anxiety can manifest in our surroundings. In the same way trauma can do a number on our bodies, it can also wreak havoc on our spaces. We have to be honest with ourselves about what got us here—it is truly the only way to see sustainable long-term success.

You can rainbow-organize the shit out of all your living spaces, but until you address the root cause, that tree will never produce fruit. It may mean professional help is needed for this journey. In my professional experience, I've seen that if this part of the equation isn't addressed, the clutter will inevitably return. The ability to manage our space will be drowned by the dark cloud of depression. Anxiety will fuel a lack of focus and deplete our motivation to maintain systems. Don't skip this part! It can be uncomfortable to admit the pain that has caused difficulty in your life, but I promise the reward is worth the work. We can never know a rainbow if we don't go through the thunderstorm first.

Recent studies have shown that clutter and stress go hand in hand. Why? Clutter feeds disordered thoughts, which increases anxiety for many people. Also closely related to clutter is procrastination, because addressing clutter is, in most of our minds, an unpleasant project. One study published in the *Journal of Personality and Social Psychology* found that those who believed their home was cluttered had increased levels of cortisol—the stress hormone—keeping them stressed throughout the day.[4] In another study, the research team found that "clutter problems led to a significant decrease in satisfaction with life."[5] Science has only scratched the surface, but the research done so far supports what I have experienced firsthand—getting a leg up on clutter not only helps improve your home life, giving you additional time to spend with your family and friends, but it also has health benefits as well. The opposite can also be true.

My own battle with depression and anxiety isn't caused by disorganization but rather the reverse—when my depression and anxiety aren't managed, my space reflects the chaos I feel in my head. It then becomes a vicious cycle in which the more anxious and overwhelmed I feel, the less intentional I am about keeping my home organized. The result: my home becomes more disorganized and messier. Until I can find a hard stop to the cycle, I spiral into a lunatic on

---

4 Darby Saxbe and Rena L. Repetti, "For Better or Worse? Coregulation of Couples' Cortisol Levels and Mood States," *Journal of Personality and Social Psychology* 98, no. 1 (2010): 92–103.

5 Joseph R. Ferrari and Catherine A. Roster, "Delaying Disposing: Examining the Relationship between Procrastination and Clutter across Generations," *Current Psychology* 37, no 2 (2018): 426–431.

the verge of a breakdown. Rage cleaning may occur, but I often lose energy after one space. As much as clutter influences mental chaos, we can take peaceful notice that the opposite is also true. When a space is serene and calming and inviting, I feel at peace mentally, more collected, and less frazzled. Not only does an organized living room make me feel better, but I can really relax and take a load off in the same space when I'm not being stared at by torturous mountains of unfolded, not-put-away laundry.

Some of you may have heard of the Life Coach Model.[6] If you haven't, lemme give you a simplified rundown. It begins with **circumstances**—neutral facts that can be proved. Circumstances lead to **thoughts** as you seek to interpret the facts. Because we are so unique, our thoughts are quite varied. Thoughts cause **feelings** with all the emotions. Feelings prompt our **actions**, whether physical or mental, but even inaction is an action. Actions cause **results**—an outcome, a consequence, or an effect, which always tie back to our first thought.

This ties into the results of having clutter and how that affects our thoughts. What is the result we want? We want an organized home where we feel relaxed and peaceful. While we can't change some circumstances—like a potentially small budget or limited time to execute—we can

---

6 See The Life Coach School website at https://thelifecoachschool.com/self-coaching-model-guide/ (accessed June 24, 2024).

change our thoughts to this truth: anyone can get organized with any budget. We also have to shift our thoughts about acquiring STUFF:

- Do I really need it?
- Is a scarcity mindset causing me to hoard?
- Do I own something similar that can do the job?
- Does this purchase align with my values like supporting small and local businesses or environmental concerns, or achieving financial goals?

We can become informed consumers by connecting our values to any purchase we make rather than connecting those buys to current emotions. I want to empower you to make choices with your money that align with your values—it really does matter.

There's a part of me that feels unworthy to write this book. Let's say it bluntly: I feel like a big, freaking phony. My dining room has not had any dining for months because it is covered in piles from school projects and extracurricular activities while I try to focus on the blinking cursor of my laptop. I am distracted by any mess; this visual clutter is screaming. We are on the other side of a spring break spent mostly at home, coupled with a few trips taken over the last few months from which we have not completely unpacked. Top it off with a demanding work schedule to keep my business afloat and my team fed and the urgency

I feel to finish this book. Where is the time to get my own house organized? Why the hell am I writing a book about organizing when I should be getting this shit show in order?

But see, that's the thing: this isn't just a book about organizing. For the love of puppies, can we stop should-ing all over ourselves? The neatness of your home does not define your worth. You don't fall within a ranking system of best to worst homemakers. All those creators on social media with their supposedly perfect spaces are stashing things in cupboards faster than an unannounced DEA drug bust. Picture that scene in *Goodfellas* when they try to get rid of all the cocaine as the cops raid the house. It's like that, but with piles of clutter.

The kicker is that even though my home may not appear organized by comparison to the previously mentioned standards, I am in fact living an organized life. Hell, I'm writing a book for Pete's sake. (Who the hell is Pete by the way? Can we say Rick's sake? Or Janet's sake?) The little piles in my spaces are not stopping me from living the life I want to live. I'm fitting in time for almost daily workouts. I'm spending time with my family. I'm taking drum lessons and practicing my French. I'd say that's living life pretty well if you ask me.

With my high standards, I certainly wouldn't mind if the piles weren't part of my regular décor, but I'm able to continue moving forward with my goals and not be held back from what is not put away. Again, I remind you, as I remind myself: *the goal is not perfection*. The goal for organizing our life is a passing grade. Your house doesn't need to look like a Restoration Hardware catalog; it doesn't need to look like anything. It just needs to be organized enough to keep the busy bus of life moving forward.

Chapter 3

WHERE DOES IT ALL COME FROM?

What does it mean to be organized? One of the biggest misconceptions in defining what it means to be organized is that most people think "organized" has to look a certain way. Organized is a FEELING, not a look or an aesthetic. The true test to being organized: Can you find what you need when you need it? If you answered yes—great, you're organized! It doesn't matter if it's rainbow-ordered or has immaculate vinyl labels. You can use cardboard boxes and masking tape with Sharpie labels to achieve the same amount of organized as those

AUDREY at Home
REESE WITHERSPOON

with matching bins and luxurious labels. You may not be bragging to your friends on Facebook about this space with old boxes and scribbled labels, but at the end of the day, it's just as easy to find a sorted category. Can you find a fork when you need to eat? Cool, sounds like your cutlery is organized. Can you find that skirt and top combo you love when getting dressed for work? No? Well, time to visit the layout of the closet. Being organized means finding what you need when you need it, and much less to do with how it looks. When we accept this approach of systems taking precedence over aesthetics, it can ease a lot of unnecessarily high expectations.

Another test of being organized is if someone else can use the space. If you're the only one who knows where anything is because none of it is labeled or you often forget the order—that's a failing grade for being organized.

This is a true challenge for all my type A mamas. If you are the only person in your household able to locate AAA batteries, this makes it harder on you, because you have to solve the Rubik's Cube anytime someone is looking for batteries in the laundry room. However, if you clearly designate a home for all batteries and label it so the other battery users in your house can become self-sufficient, there's the easier-to-manage-life part.[7] There's likely to be at least one or two

7 Does not apply to toddlers who can't read or spouses who refuse to read.

in your household who are willing to learn how to fish for themselves. Only half of the spaces we organize for our clients make it to the social media showcase, which means we have organized hundreds of spaces that aren't perfectly picturesque but still left the client FEELING organized. Their space felt manageable. They had clarity on what lived where, and the spaces were labeled so other users could find what they needed when they needed it.

Something important can be learned from the spaces and systems that ARE working in your house. Think about the areas of your home that seem to hold themselves together with rational levels of effort. You can learn much about yourself and your habits by looking closely at those spaces. Do you need to have exposed storage bins in order to put it back where it goes? What categories are best sustained with this type of layout?

Keep in mind that the more steps involved in putting an item away in its "home," the less likely it will make it there. This can be a hard balance to strike when you aren't the only one who uses the space, as different systems work for different people. In the end, making it as easy and clear as possible is perhaps the better bet to get everyone to buy in and be a part of the maintenance portion.

We adore all the gorgeous baskets and bin clip labels, but what matters first is how you feel in the space. This test is incredibly present when I ask clients what space they want to prioritize as the most impactful one to organize first. It's always the one space where they can't find anything: the one area that feels like a complete disaster, where there's no clarity to what is where or what should be where.

CLUTTER VS. STUFF

Your stuff is your stuff. Meaning it's yo' shit. It's the clothes you wear, the things you do, the items you collect in your home. Not all stuff is clutter, but all clutter is stuff—stuff that may not be serving your life anymore. Your stuff can be awesome. It can be your Air Force One collection, the starting lineup of your favorite baseball team in bobbleheads, your board games for family Friday nights, or your workout gear.

Your stuff may from time to time be out of place or away from its home—the place it lives when you're not using it. Just because it's out doesn't mean it's automatically clutter that needs to be purged. It may simply mean you were just too tired or busy to put it back. It happens all the time—multiple times a day, in fact. When was the last time you retrieved a cup out of the cupboard, poured a glass of water, immediately drank it, and then washed it and put it right back in the cupboard? If you answered last week, I can't imagine why you need this book because that is some impressive micromanagement you are rockin'!

Despite the minimalist images strewn across social media platforms, you are allowed to actually have stuff in your house. It's absolutely normal if your stuff hangs out on your counter or a chair sometimes, or even most of the time. Don't demonize the things you use in your day-to-day life—the enemy isn't your stuff. The downfall, the transition from stuff to clutter, is having too much stuff—more than you have room to store or time to maintain. Your stuff has now piled into so many layers, you don't know where to start even if you have the motivation to clean up. This fed-up, I-don't-know-where-to-start feeling may in fact have been the epiphany that motivated you to purchase this book.

I've blamed my insane roommates, aka my family, for the difficulties of managing clutter. You may do the same, but let's not pretend the clutter is all their fault. Taking our share of responsibility for the mayhem in which we find ourselves is truly illuminating. It will help us shift the narrative with our roommates so we don't waste time pointing fingers but instead establish a shared responsibility everyone has a part in maintaining—period.

It doesn't matter who is more responsible; if you live there, you have an invested interest in creating order. On the other hand, if you are a solo act in the chaos, it's equally important for you to find accountability in a kind, gentle way. Check in with yourself. What parts of the equation that led to a house of clutter do you recognize, and which parts need a little more digging into?

ALVREZ
THE Ladies' Room READER
CONARI PRESS
Century
BYGONES
LaVyrle Spencer
PUTNAM
THE ADVENTURES OF HAJJI BABA OF ISPAHAN
MORIER
KITTY KELLEY
ELIZABETH TAYLOR
John Updike
THE MUSIC SCHOOL
Alfred A Knopf

TYPES OF CLUTTER KEEPERS

1. Shopper Sally

The Shopper Sally type, clutter-keeper, cuts me deep, like a dagger being twisted through my heart. Truth be told, I have no fewer than six boxes in my entryway eagerly waiting to be unpacked. It's like Christmas on my doorstep at least once a week, though it's not entirely personal—half the time it's organizing supplies. Even so, you should see how excited I get over a new label tape color combo or nifty hand tool. The other half of the time the boxes contain a new workout outfit, a board game for my kids, or some other tempting item the Instagram ads tricked me into buying.

Contrary to perception, a professional organizer is not the same as a minimalist. Most of us don't limit ourselves to owning only five pairs of shoes or three books or keeping as little as possible stored in our homes. Not to knock the lifestyle choice minimalists make, but I view it in the same way I view a Buddhist monk. I have mad respect for their sacrifice and devotion to their beliefs, but I feel more of a "love that journey for you" vibe.

I love shopping. It has been a joyful pastime for me since I was a preteen. Back then your parent would dump you at the local mall with your two best friends with $20 burning a hole in your pocket and limitless hours to waste perusing the racks of every store. There was no social media or smartphone to consume our time. These were the days when I had to save a quarter to call my mom—on the relics called pay phones—to come pick us up when we were out of money. Every fall brought back-to-school shopping, and even though I could only shop at Mervyn's, the thrill of a new pair of shoes did not waver. The dopamine would hit, and for someone who struggled with self-confidence (like most teenage girls), wearing a new pair of jeans was just the boost I needed on the first day of school.

Now the same thrilling experience can be recreated anytime, anywhere from the palm of my hand. With the tap of one finger, boxes can be delivered from anywhere in the world. I shudder typing this, realizing how easy it is to consume. The point is that it is incredibly easy to acquire more. For those of us who love a sale or a discount code and get our little serotonin boost from the activity, it's not only easy to shop; it's also addictive.

Advertisers know this, so their algorithms track our online behavior in order to target specific products to us. They learn what hobbies we enjoy, where we like to hang out, and what shows we watch—all in an effort to sell us more stuff. If you spend any time online, there's no hiding from it. Considering that the majority of marketing and advertising for my company is online means that I spend a fair bit of time there each week. I can pass on the cookie and say no to a cocktail, but when a snazzy pair of new high-top sneakers show up like a thirst trap, I'm checkin' them out.

While I may not have an overflow of stuff (take it from

me, don't ask my husband), everything I add certainly creates more time I have to spend managing stuff to honor the "one in, one out rule." There are boxes to be unpacked weekly and arrangements to be made in closets and drawers to accommodate the incoming goods. In my defense, it feels like something that has become a constant task since having kids. I didn't even order from Amazon until I had children, when the convenience gear shifted into an all-time high. I was so sleep-deprived and desperate. Then I added in a changing and demanding business with ongoing supply needs—travel vacuums, stepladders, hand tools, and more—and the ordering never seems to stop.

2. Procrastinator Paula

The latest season of *Bridgerton* or *Yellowstone* seems so much more appealing than going through our bathroom drawers and clearing clutter. So we put it off. Then we put it off again. And then we put it off again, and before we realize it a year or maybe years have passed and we've never gotten around to the project we promised ourselves we were going to conquer.

Listen up, procrastinators: I am with you. My social calendar seems so much more entertaining than folding laundry or attacking that mystery pile in the garage. I can delay getting it done with the best of them.

Take my high school biology bug project. We were given months, I mean multiple months, to collect, identify, freeze, and mount 10 different species of insects. To this day I have an aversion to creepy crawlies, so it's not a surprise that at the immature age of 13 I basically ignored this project and its due date. I neither thought through what would happen if I didn't do the project, nor attempted to scheme a way around it. I just pretended it didn't exist, and I didn't do it.

Then the due date arrived. Everyone in the class turned in varying degrees of effort. We had the A-plus Allisons with bugs so perfectly preserved we could have displayed them in a museum. We had the D-minus Dannys whose projects looked like they killed a couple of ants on the way, grabbed some tape, and strapped them down half alive on the way to school. I avoided being called on until my teacher pulled me aside after third period and asked me where my bug project was. My face immediately swelled red with embarrassment because I hadn't thought of an excuse and was ultimately mortified that I had given it zero effort for no good reason. She called my mom to inform her of the situation, and that night I reluctantly scrounged together a few bugs to turn in something the next day.

Did I learn a valuable lesson from this scenario? I learned that procrastination did not prevent the task from needing to be completed. I filed that experience away knowing I never wanted that sinking feeling in my stomach again.

Fast-forward to today, when I see projects wait months for my attention. Sure, I can blame my full schedule or packed to-do list, but even when I slow down—like this week, with my kids home during spring break—I know my makeup drawer needs rehab or the utility room could use a reset. So what do I do? I deem any and everything else to be more important, even though I know the stress relief that clearing those spaces would give me.

This comes from someone who technically could turn any cleaning or organizing project into content for her business, yet still finds excuses to delay at home. I truly believe we have an uncanny ability to make something seem so much more daunting and exhaustive than it really is. Catastrophizing can be an art form. We have to remind ourselves how proud we will be once we have tackled the project and how gratified we will feel when it is complete. Instead, we overanalyze and overplan and exaggerate the size of the project so much that it becomes the size of Everest, and we feel we can never conquer it.

My Procrastinator Paulas out there need to read, listen, or just freaking google what it means to "eat the frog"—do the one huge, daunting task first, and live the rest of the day on the high of knowing what you have accomplished. Another metaphor to ask yourselves: "How do you eat an elephant?" Well, one bite at a time, of course. Don't get lost in the process of how you are ever going to eat an entire elephant—or in our case, how you are ever going to organize your closet. Focus on one bite at a time—so grab the ketchup or your fave condiment, pour some on, and *bon appetit*!

3. Busy Betty

Betty keeps a full calendar. A happy hour meet-up with colleagues on the reg, a monthly book club digesting the latest beach read, pickleball practice with her bae, and she replies "yes" to almost all other social engagements that come her way. This girl doesn't do downtime. To schedule a dinner date with Betty, you better be ready to book six to eight weeks in advance. Another iteration is the Busy Betty whose kids keep a full schedule from practices to recitals to after-school scout meetings. This Betty is an Uber driver, DoorDasher, and Instacart rep wrapped into a single person.

My beloved mother-in-law, God rest her soul, was a Busy Betty. She was never home longer than the hours she slept or to grab a change of clothes. Not only did she work full time as a cardio ICU nurse at a prestigious hospital group here in Houston, but in her sarcastically implied down time she also volunteered for the Texas State Medical Brigade, which is basically an army of nurses who wear camo and save lives when there is a state of emergency or a natural disaster. If that wasn't enough, she was an involved grandmother and fierce friend to those in her circle. You could call her up anytime and say, "Hey, want to grab coffee and go to Target," and if she wasn't on duty she was always there with bells on. She lived a beautiful and full life outside of her home, which made it hard to keep up *inside* her home.

When you don't give yourself time for a reset, it is impossible to maintain any organizing systems. There is no exact division of time to follow, but you have to assess what it would take to feel you are able to maintain your space without causing added stress. Maybe it's every other weekend without plans to reset, or at least one full day a week—it really depends on your obligations and the chaos it ensues. Know also that there are seasons that require more focus at home than others.

When I was single and living in an apartment, I only needed half a day to recover and reset my week, and it usually ended up being a Sunday afternoon. With a busy young family, I can easily fill every weekend with cleaning and organizing. At the very least, one weekend day I schedule absolutely nothing on the calendar—nada, zilch, nothin'. I don't want to get dressed or do anything except prepare for the week ahead. On some occasions when this schedule block isn't possible or work is heavy and requires my attention, I will clear a few hours Monday evening to pick up the slack. Not surprisingly, my husband is a lot like his precious mum. He loooooves to plan all the things, says "yes" to any and all invitations, music lessons, workouts, and church activities—he wants to do it all.

Sometimes I find it hard to choose between spending time with my family or setting my workload for the week ahead. This past weekend is a prime example. Our family just had a full week at home for a holiday. The house was completely destroyed; my kids demolished any resemblance of the organizing systems in all their areas of play.

Just getting them to school on this postapocalyptic Monday was a shit show, to put it lightly. No one could find what they wanted to wear, school folders were forgotten, and we patched together a rough day of survival. This is what all my weeks would be like if I didn't allow the space on my schedule to reset. When you keep a calendar packed with obligations, nothing is put away, mail is never opened, food expires, and projects go undone. The busyness can bleed into performance at your job and stall advances in your career or growth opportunities in your business. It can look like personal affairs are going unaccounted for—late payments on bills, oversights in insurance renewals, and maybe even delays in filing your taxes. Though you may be able to put disorganization out of sight and out of mind for the short term, it will eventually build up to a stressful burden that haunts you every time you have an unscheduled minute. This stress will follow you and occupy your thoughts and drain your energy. Ignoring your responsibilities is an unnecessary drain on your energy—energy that could be brought to the next fun gathering where you celebrate the freedom of having dominated those boring tasks.

4. Collector Carol

When Carol loves the fit of a T-shirt, she goes back and buys it in every color available. She can't just have one Spode Christmas plate; Carol wants the full collection even if she will never use the full set in a single holiday season. Carol

Soggy Doggy
CATAN
TROUBLE
CATAN
OPERATION
Hippos
MAGNETIC PATTERNING KIT
EAT IT!

loves collecting—fashion, housewares, vintage phones, or funky chairs (or is that just me?). She might be a sentimental collector—every picture her child has ever drawn and every piece of schoolwork they've ever done. Thirteen years of school later, this collection amounts to containers and containers of worksheets and art and projects.

Perhaps you have saved every cork from every bottle of wine you shared with your spouse, and now 25 years into marriage, you could build a dining table with them. (If you do in fact build a dining table with those corks, then please share the photo.) However, if you haven't figured out the next step nor are you sure how to incorporate your collections into your home style, you might be collecting for the sake and satisfaction of collecting.

It's possible everyone is a collector of certain categories—but Carol applies this habit to most things. The issue is an abundance of stuff that accumulates quickly and takes lots of valuable space to store. There are too many shoes, too many dishes, too many somethings. So many somethings that Carol needs a storage unit (or two or three) just to hold on to all these items. It is here that the collecting becomes a burden—in time spent shuffling these things around, and in the cost associated with storing them.

As you may have noticed, there is not a hard and fast you-can-keep-two-plates-per-person kind of rule, but rather you can save as much as you can store. You have a closet to accommodate one T-shirt in every color? Cool, buy away.

You don't? Well, time to consider where the right line for keeps is for you. Physical barriers like the current size of your closet are the best way to set boundaries. Someone in New York probably has fewer clothes than someone in Texas because, like everything else in this state, the closets are bigger here too. Hey, live where you want, and if you want a closet the size of a house in the middle of Nebraska, that's your business.

My kids love the show *Bluey* on Disney, and it's definitely a favorite of mine from the category of kids shows. I hate the children's programming loaded with sirens, and I am not a fan of the child-targeted staged overdramatized scenarios on YouTube. One of the recent episodes of *Bluey* we watched was the one where the two kids, Bluey and Bingo, had to go through all their stuffed animals and decide which ones to keep and which to chuck or donate. Ultimately, they wanted to keep them all—every kid ever, am I right? But the lesson they learned in their process of letting go of the toys they no longer played with was that essentially if everything is special, then nothing is special. Who knew these lessons could be learned—or relearned—for adults as well?

When you have all the sports jerseys for every player on your favorite team, it diminishes the uniqueness of your favorite player's jersey. Collector Carol has the tendency to find a favorite type of product or style of shoe and want to multiply them or buy backups. This is not inherently bad, as long as we have the space to store it and it fits the budget we are comfortable spending. We have to learn where the line is for us—often determined by that physical barrier of space we have to store—and which categories need a smidge more discernment. For me, I am a sneakerhead, but I gotta keep my love for Nike Air Force Ones in check. When the world checked out in 2020, I realized comfort is king and heels have made fewer than five appearances since. Gone are the days of my twenties when I ran around in heels so that my height was marginally average instead of the topic of every conversation with someone new ("Oh man, you're short!" Thank you, Captain Obvious). Now I'm in my DGAF era, where I feel most myself and most comfy in my latest Adidas Gazelle kicks. (In all honesty, I also love the adoration from fellow sneaker lovers on my unique color combo or how I styled my outfit around them.) To my credit card's demise, I find it hard to resist any release, including any animal print of any color. A note of encouragement and caution to us collectors out there: let's love our collections but limit them to what fits in our stage of life today and remember to keep the special ones, special.

5. Overwhelmed Olivia

Olivia is a little bit of everyone mixed into one overwhelmed, anxiety-drenched mess. *Inside Out 2* gave us a great depiction of what is going on mentally when we let anxiety take the driver's seat. Maybe you saw a bit of yourself in all of these personas—Shopper Sally, Procrastinator

Paula, Busy Betty, and Collector Carol. I have seen myself in each of them during certain seasons of my life. The purpose of listing these descriptions was to better understand the areas in which we get in our own way in our quest of becoming more organized.

It's not easy to hold up a mirror and have a heart-to-heart conversation with ourselves. Vulnerability and honesty come in hefty doses for this much-needed inner dialogue. I certainly don't want this to lead us back to the shame and guilt we left behind, but rather give us a better understanding of our shortcomings so we can make any needed adjustments.

It's like getting a previous copy of a test back. Some people might be okay with knowing the grade and moving on with their life—yet the real learning moment comes from seeing where we made mistakes on the exam, looking into our thought process leading to answers, and understanding how we need to redirect the next time for the correct answer. How can we truly learn from our mistakes if we don't see the answers we got wrong?

This exercise is similar. Going through these personifications gives us all the possibilities so we can see where we may have fallen behind in the past, and then we can strive to be the best versions of ourselves in the future. No shade and no shame intended—only a deeper look into our humanness and a reminder of what to keep an eye on in our daily decisions. I have absolutely been each of these characters at some point in my life, and you probably have too.

Chapter 4

DON'T TOSS EVERYTHING!

Before you roll up those sleeves and throw everything you see into a garbage bag, here are a few points to prepare for success and prep for your journey to an organized life. Are you ready to get started?

A SIMPLIFIED LIFE
EMILY LEY
EMILY HENDERSON
STYLED

THE BEFORE-YOU-CAN-ORGANIZE ORGANIZING STEPS

1. Do NOT Buy Products First

It can be tempting to rush over to Target and load up your cart with every pretty bin you see. Instead, I ask this of you: please DON'T buy all the pretty boxes just yet. We've all been the victim of an alluring organizing basket as the initial inspiration to organize a space in our home. I have even succumbed to a good deal online and purchased an organizing item before I had a plan in place for how it could truly serve me. You know what ends up happening nine times out of ten, though? I don't find any way for this item to function in my home and it sits boxed up.

As organizers, we can make many inferences about product needs using the listed inventory and measurements of an area coupled with our years of expertise. It is how we are able to prebuild a suggested product list before the real organizing begins. There are times we consider a workaround or make do with what's available. However, in cases of DIY organizing, the best assessment of product needs comes after the application of our proprietary ROAR (Remove, Organize, Analyze, Return) Organized Design Process is completed. Without these tools—which you will learn soon—I highly recommend walking through the entire process before investing in products to complete your space.

It's like having the instructions to build an outdoor

swing set. Could you build the swing set without directions? Maybe? Probably? But something will definitely end up backward, and I bet a few things won't line up right. Wouldn't having directions make for a lot less cursing and a lot more lined-up corners? Having the full picture before choosing bins and baskets also saves you total time on the project. You won't have to run back and forth to the store with returns or exchanges, and therefore, you'll save those precious hours as well as the gas money.

2. Get Your Crew on Board

An integral part of success for your organized life journey is gaining the buy-in from everyone in your household that we talked about earlier. Yes, even your dog should be on board with a toy bin, but probably not your cat, Snicklefits, who doesn't give a rat's tail about what you're doing to organize the house. It's imperative to at least broach this conversation with your roommates, whether or not they are related to you. You will soon discover their responses will vary from enthusiastic to indifferent. Don't take it too personally if others in your household are not as excited as you are about your goal to give clutter the middle finger. I'm sure any toddlers or teenagers will be less than interested in the whole idea. You may even have a spouse who is apathetic or perhaps even against this endeavor entirely. Your partner not being on board with this lifestyle adjustment is no reason not to move forward, though some accommodations may be required. For example, certain spaces could be off-limits when it comes to their belongings—which is completely fair. There is nothing more detrimental to getting your partner on board than organizing their stuff without their permission.

We have learned through an organizing project gone wrong that absolutely no one likes their stuff messed with when they have not given explicit permission. This is exactly why, if someone calls asking us to organize for their parent or spouse or child and the person whose stuff is the clutter in question is not on board with the idea, the answer is, "I'm so sorry, but this isn't the right fit."

The best response to the naysayers is to show them what it looks like to live in a more organized manner. They will quickly see that you're less anxious and feel more in control once your life is organized. The lead-by-example idea truly works in this instance. It may not be something they change their mind about overnight, but, in time, they might see the benefits of what you are doing. Will they wake up one day and say, "Me too"? Eh, who knows? Truly, there are some people in the world who appear oblivious to clutter. It's hard to relate to these robots. They aren't able to imagine life differently because they claim not to see a problem to begin with. If they did, then they'd see what they are missing. I guess it's like if I had never had coffee before, I wouldn't ever know how amazing life is with coffee. (And I can testify that in a life after coffee, it has become one of my favorite parts of every single day.)

The rule of living by example holds true for everyone in your household, even your kids. If you think about it: when we have a fit because our kids' rooms look like a natural disaster aftermath, the harsh reality comes when we consider what our own rooms look like. Are we setting the example we want them to live? This truth has been a lightbulb moment for many parents, including me. It started when my oldest was just a toddler. At first it seemed easier to manage her clothes and her toys, so keeping her nursery in order was a preference over keeping order in my own room. I don't think I realized how unfair it was when I would scold her in elementary years for not tidying up after herself when I was guilty of leaving my shoes in the middle of the floor as well. As always, I'm not wanting to throw shade here but rather give some perspective so we can gain better insight into ourselves and be the leaders our household needs for this journey.

3. Set Aside the Time

The time to accomplish the goal is going to vary drastically based on your duties and responsibilities. Do you have a full-time job or care for a relative? If the answer is yes, give yourself grace and space to manage this endeavor. The biggest mistake would be setting yourself up for failure based on unrealistic expectations and then being discouraged by your lack of progress. This will only stifle your confidence and make the end goal seem further away.

It can be difficult to see the changes day to day. Instead, think about where you were last week or compare the changes to where you were a month ago, and you can truly see change happening. A sacrifice of some kind is needed in order to see substantial growth in becoming more organized. It may look like a reduced social schedule or a few personal days off work. Heck, if you can take a week off from work, think how impactful that could be. And if that is not in the cards, the evenings and weekends are where you channel your energy. No matter how tempting it is to sleep in on the weekends and catch up on the latest Netflix binge, you'll need to channel that fed-up energy to keep your mind focused on the goal. It's true this is easier said than done when you've been working or caring for kids all week, so give yourself balance and reward for progress made. I joke that if I could send my kids and spouse away for a week and hire a small army, I'd be able to focus on reorganizing and deep-cleaning—but alas, my manifesting that mantra hasn't brought this to fruition quite yet.

4. Make Change Your Number One Priority

This is the secret sauce to the sandwich of getting organized. When my editor gave me a final deadline to meet, I had no choice but to buckle down with my writing schedule. I knew this book had to take the first and best energy from me. There were some mishaps along the way, including storm power outages and health concerns resulting in surgery mid-edit, but my number one priority remained this book. That even meant taking an extended break from client projects so I could focus my creative energy on my number one priority, this book.

When you have a sole focus, encouraged by the fed-up-with-this-crap attitude, you can keep yourself on track. Put reminders in your phone calendar, stick Post-its on your bathroom mirror—whatever it takes to remember that you are getting your shit together so you can have an easier, more peaceful life is your "earth in the window." You may have heard that before: it's an *Apollo 13* reference the astronauts used when they were discouraged by the challenges of their mission. There they were floating out in the middle of space, and the spaceship kept breaking down. Cue the line, "Houston, we have a problem." They were reminded by their NASA guides stationed in my beloved H-town to focus on the Earth view they could see out the window of the space module, which acted as their constant visual reminder of what the goal was: a safe return home to Earth. Maybe that earth in the window for you is hosting the next book club night or simply not sweating every time the doorbell rings. When you identify your end game, you can stay focused on the priority at hand.

When I was focusing on writing this book, I kept a writing schedule of either one hour or 1,000 words every single day, whatever came first. A similar version for organizing could be one hour or one space, even as small as one drawer.

When you approach organizing your kitchen one drawer or cabinet at a time, it can break down the daunting task into manageable steps. Get a friend to do this challenge with you so you can both have an accountability partner to check in with and maybe even share ideas about the spaces you are organizing. If this friend happens to be a neighbor, maybe you could alternate helping each other out so that you can really get the ball rolling. It's true that momentum picks up as you feel progress. As your organizing muscle grows stronger, so does your confidence. You are gonna organize the shit out of your life, not for the purposes of bragging to your friends on social media (I mean if you want to, by all means, show off your hard work), but to truly create an easier flow in your life so you can get back to fun and freedom.

GETTING STARTED

On this short list, number one is the easiest—all you have to do is to NOT do something. Don't shop for organizing products—the end, and you can check the box on one. Number two isn't too bad. It may not yield willing sidekicks in the organizing process, but having a conversation with your family or roommates to get everyone on the same page is the way to forge a path to organizing success.

For most, the hard part sinks in at number three. Setting aside the time is truly one of the toughest parts. Life is so busy and full of things to do and people to see and, well, ya gotta eat too. This is what makes carving out extra time seem daunting. You feel like you have none to spare before you have even started. However, I promise you can find it. With two young girls to raise, a household to run, and a business to keep afloat, it seemed impossible to fathom how I would ever write this book. How could I find time in what felt like an already packed schedule to churn out a freakin' book with over 40,000 words?

Don't get me wrong: there were some serious delays and challenges, and more than once I wanted to give up (like every other week). Both business and personal matters got in the way and stole my energy and attention, but I persevered and found a rhythm for writing that worked for me. I won't be writing this book forever until the end of time, although sometimes it feels like it will take that long—just like you won't be organizing spaces forever.

Earning a passing organized life grade isn't the easiest or the hardest thing you'll ever do. It will take a chunk of dedicated time and focused effort for a period of time. It may be as little as a couple of weeks or a few months, depending on your current responsibilities, but I promise it's attainable. Writing this book took me several years, so don't be discouraged by a changing timeline. I stopped and started over twice since 2020, during the pandemic. My fed-up energy was knowing I wanted to reach more than just the clients who could afford me. I wanted to have this conversation with you, which was hard to do if we didn't live in the same city and had the budget to hire my team. That reward of changing peoples' lives and the feelings they have around clutter and creating realistic, organized goals has been my Earth in the window—so is getting organized to better enjoy your life yours?

GET IT
SUZANNE SYZ

Chapter 5

LET'S ROAR!

If you've made it this far, great! We know you're not wiping anyone else's ass on the daily or battling a health crisis, which means you have the bandwidth to undertake an organizing project. Don't panic. Take a deep breath. I did not say we were going to organize your entire home in one day. We're going to break this down into bite-sized pieces in a clear process that almost everyone can understand.

Let's remember—first things first. Rome wasn't built in a day. For our purposes, you cannot organize your entire home in a single weekend. Sorry to burst your bubble, but it's important for you to set up reasonable expectations from the start. Perhaps if you live in a 480-square-foot studio in NYC, but I'm going to guess that's not most of you.

Now, I don't imagine you're just lying around looking for ways to fill your time, either. You have a job or a family or a hobby or likely all of the above calling for your attention. No matter your average weekly schedule, one thing I know for sure is that you will have to intentionally carve out time to reach your organizing goals. A Sunday with zero plans won't just magically reveal itself, nor will you suddenly be bursting with energy to organize #allthethings. Quite the contrary: most of us are so exhausted from the previous week and so anxious about starting a new one that we spend our Sunday comatose on the couch, watching hours of eye-opening documentaries because we simply can't will ourselves to do much more than fold a single basket of laundry, forget putting that away in closets. This brings us to the first task at hand.

SCHEDULE AN APPOINTMENT

Schedule the appointment with yourself to spend active, focused time organizing. You read that right: open the calendar on your smartphone (or your paper planner if you're an elder millennial plus), and make a daily appointment for at least one hour to dedicate to this process. Make it daily, because at least one or two of those days are gonna turn into a dumpster fire and you will likely only make it happen four

or five times a week. At least one of those days you're gonna look at your reminder and think, nope.

Choose a time in the day when . . .

- **It's humanly possible.** For example, not during the witching hour of 5:00 to 6:00 p.m. if that's when your toddler is the neediest human on the planet. If that's the time of day when you're battling for bath time with the tiny dictator who lives in your house, it is not the ideal hour to organize your closet. This also means that scheduling your organizing time in the middle of your workday, even if you work from home, may not make sense. Your boss will notice if you have a daily doctor appointment from 2:00 to 3:00 p.m. on your shared calendar with the location of your living room. You may have to give up a little TV time or wake up a little earlier to find a time that works consistently.

- **You are not mentally and physically depleted.** This is tricky, because I can already feel your panic as you ask, When the heck is that supposed to be? Some people are night owls and are able to start or focus on a task at 8:00 in the evening. Me, on the other hand, I absolutely love getting ready for bed at that time and being in bed by 9:00 p.m., doing my Duolingo French lesson, maybe a Calm sleep meditation, or a few pages of my latest fiction, and then *bonne nuit* by 9:30 p.m.

    There are certain times during the day when you

bring your best self for a workout, and there may be a different time of day when you are able to bring your A game for a mental task like writing. It's the same with organizing. Carve out the hour wherever it makes the most sense for you, your energy trajectory, and your schedule to give organizing your best effort.

These two elements are of the utmost importance. Without an honest conversation with yourself about scheduling the time, it's impossible to expect the time to appear. This is the downfall a lot of us face with any lofty goal. Heck, this book wouldn't exist if I didn't take this approach to be able to write it. It had nothing to do with my desire or passion for writing; it was just a simple fact that if I didn't schedule appointments to focus solely on writing when my freshest creative energy was available, then it wouldn't happen. I had to ignore clients, maybe even my kids, and other temptations like scrolling social media and go all in on the laptop and write. I had to write with a deadline on the calendar and the TV unplugged. This is the same dedication you need to bring to get organized. Block out distractions, ignore temptations, and give organizing the energy it needs.

Did you schedule those appointments yet? You think I'm just being metaphorical, don't you? Well, doll, if you haven't gathered by now, I mean literally schedule those appointments—Google Calendar is my favorite, because it will pop up like an annoying text to remind you of the goal.

Make the appointment consistent with the two factors we discussed earlier: when it's humanly possible, and when you are not mentally and physically depleted.

When it comes to my prayer time or a workout, I'm an early bird. I do those before my kids can disrupt my routine or my clients need my attention urgently. As for the best writing time for me, I learned after some trial and error that it's actually the end of the day, right before I eat dinner or when my kiddos are in the bath—that is the span of time I am able to focus on writing. It's on my calendar every day, but I also know I'm good for it maybe five times a week. The daily reminder is there to keep my focus on my ultimate goal. It is my earth in the window, just as designing your organized life is your earth in the window. How long you will need to set these appointments is dependent on the number of spaces and your commitment. It could take you a week to complete your closet; it could take a month. This is your timetable to create.

THE ROAR PROCESS

No matter the type of space, the ROAR process works—whether it's a tool drawer in your kitchen or the chaos in your pantry. I'm trying to make fetch happen by referring to a "tool drawer" here as an example instead of a "junk drawer." Why? If you call it junk, then guess what ends up in there? You guessed right: it's junk if that's what you call it. If you call it tools, you might even see a pair of scissors end up in there.

Our proprietary ROAR Organized Design Process has taken 10 years to formulate and perfect. The acronym has changed at least half a dozen times. We have practiced the method with hundreds of our clients, and we are pretty darn proud of it. Now we're ready to share this high-impact Organized Design Process with you so you can understand and implement how we do what we do.

So what does "high-impact organization" even mean? Since we may only have one or two days to completely transform a client's space, we want to make the most of our time, effort, and impact. First, we help clients decide which is the right space to prioritize. Then we determine the right size team for their project. One client may benefit from one-on-one assistance, while others might be ready to tackle several projects and a team of four is the womanpower required to get it done.

Most of our clients have an inclination for starting an organization project but never seem to be able to *finish*. Others thought they finished a space, yet a couple of weeks later the thread unravels quickly to reveal errors in the system. High-impact organization is THOROUGH. It can't be done halfway. We all know that if you put in half effort, you reap half results. We want our organization techniques to not just solve a problem in the short term, but to build habits that last for months and years. Tweaking the space will be required over time as needs change and as life chapters unfold, but ultimately a system is established to act as a foundation, just like the foundation of a home. It provides the basis of a home that may need updates as the needs of the occupants arise and change.

The goal is to equip each one of you with an organized space that suits your lifestyle and habit tendencies. Where do you get undressed each day? That's the place your hamper should live. Do you wear your workout shoes every day? Your shoes need a bottom shelf location in the closet or a space by the door. Are you an avid baker? You need clear containers for staple baking goods to help you easily find the needed ingredients. These are just a sampling of all the questions and options we help you analyze to curate the perfect organized system in each space.

Remove, Organize, Analyze, Return. This is our ROAR Organizing Process. I highly encourage you to try this out on a tiny space like your tool (formerly known as junk) drawer. Doing this process on a small space allows you to see it through to the end in a short span. You'll gain confidence in how to run through the process and gain perspective on any hiccups you may have in larger spaces. Are you ready to ROAR?

Remove

Remove all items from the area being organized. That's right: empty the pantry, closet, garage, office, or playroom to its barest stage. Every last dust bunny should be removed. Nothing should be left unturned. This gives us a clean slate from which to work.

Remove is always the first step. You have to remove #allthethings from the space—basically, pretend you're moving and need to empty everything out. This allows a fresh start to begin organizing. As a note of caution: it always seems to get worse before it gets WAY better. Seeing every item pulled out can feel overwhelming, but don't panic. This is part of the process. By removing #alltheth-ings, you are then able to imagine how the space should function—instead of how it came together by default—and create a system with purpose.

No matter the space, large or small, remove is always step one.

Organize

Organize every item into a category. For example, food groups for the pantry, hobbies and tools for the garage, Barbies and Legos for the playroom. We want to see each sorted group put together. This is the only way to know how much room is needed for office supplies when we see out in the open how many office supplies there really are. This guideline is part of the professional organizer philosophy of "like should be stored with like." Your dresses should live together with other dresses, your power bars want to bunk with their other power bar friends, and

markers
markers
embellishments
poms
poms

your kiddo's trains are best enjoyed and played with when found in one location.

How granular you get when organizing your stuff into individual categories is your preference. Do you need to separate dresses by sleeve style and length? One consideration is the quantity in question. If you have five dresses in total, no need to separate further. If you have something closer to 25? Then it can be helpful to separate the category further by sleeve length. You do what works for your lifestyle.

Analyze

Analyze each category. How can you know which jeans you love the most until all your jeans are in front of you? We admit that analyzing can be tough. There are hard decisions to be made about keepsakes, clothes, toys, kitchen gadgets, and more. This is where the work really kicks into high gear of purging down to the items we use and love the most. Don't lose faith in the process if this is where the overwhelm sets in. This part can be daunting, but I believe in you!

Some questions to pose to yourself when analyzing items in each category: Does [item in question] serve a purpose in my life? Do I use it or love it? Sneakers? Use them. Vintage pink clock radio? Love it. And most importantly, do I have space in my life for this item?

I want to help you walk through this analysis process. Some have even called me an "expert question poser." If you can phone a friend, it's genuinely great to have an unbiased third party to help you make these decisions. Does this color shirt look good with my skin tone? Do I really need to keep the bread maker I haven't used once in five years? Having an unemotional person of influence can be beneficial in the analyzation portion. This helps avoid analysis paralysis. Take breaks and keep your fave tunes playing or put on a fun podcast so you don't hit a wall with decision fatigue.

Return

Return all "keep" items to their newly labeled home. All right, you've come a long way, friend! You have removed, organized, and analyzed #allthethings. Everything you've decided to keep has earned a rightful place in your space. Every pair of shoes, every memorabilia box trinket, every file will have a home where it will live when not in use.

As you begin to return things to the empty space, you will find categories that may not belong in the space they came from. Instead, they are better used and accessed in another space of your home. There are a few occasions where you may have one home for an item but must break up the rest of the category. For example, I feed my dogs in my kitchen area with some of their dog food stored, but their back-up bags of food are stored in the garage. This is not the norm for most categories, but it's something to consider if the spot where the item is used is restricted and the whole category doesn't fit. Another example of this is shoes: a majority of shoes are stored in each person's respective closet. However, we also have a few slip-on, hurry-out-the-door shoes by the back door, which is also our laundry/utility/mudroom. There is a designated spot for shoes so when we do get our ducks in a row in this space, it's clear how many we can store and where they go. It's also important to prioritize the highest-use categories in the most accessible locations. If you're working in a bathroom, return the most-used items to the easiest-to-reach shelves or drawers and the lesser-used items on the highest shelves or in the back. This again takes into account your lifestyle and habits to know which categories need to be accessed most often.

And the finale of return, honey, is that it MUST be labeled. It can be anything from hand-lettered labels to vinyl Cricut labels to label maker tape labels. Hell, it can be a torn piece of masking tape and a Sharpie—this is not a design competition; just get it labeled. Trust me: you think you'll remember what that bin in the attic is holding, but why use up more brain cells when we can just label and you'll never need to memorize it?

IT'S NOT FINISHED UNLESS IT'S LABELED

There is no such thing as overlabeling. The only exception is if your space looks like my six-year-old's room, where every door is covered with a sheet of stickers. That may indeed

PIONEER
since 1851
BUTTERMILK
DRY GOODS
BAKING MIXES
JIFFY
corn muffin mix
TORTILLAS
EXTRA LONG ENRICHED RICE
ORGANIC CANE SUGAR
ALL PURPOSE FLOUR
KRUSTEAZ PANCAKE MIX

qualify as too many. What I mean is that you should label as many categories and reminders as you can to make your life easier to manage and to find what you need when you need it faster.

Labeling truly completes an organized space and gives you that finally finished feeling. I have a three-panel light switch in the kitchen, and I even label that so that anyone in my kitchen—including me!—never forgets which switch controls connect to which set of lights. Labeling also gives clarity to everyone else in the home. It's hard to miss the chargers and cords bin when it obviously has the label "Cords & Chargers" on it. Note I said "hard to miss," not "impossible to miss." Your below-reading-level toddlers and those who refuse to read what's right in front of their face (**cough** spouses **cough**) will be the exceptions to the aforementioned obvious labeling. I can only offer the additional suggestion of labeling with photos and VERY BOLD LETTERING where helpful.

Let's talk about finding your labeling style. There are lots of fun options! While your aesthetic may prefer a vinyl custom style, your budget and time may only allow for label tape style. This is where KISS comes in: Keep It Simple, Stupid. Don't wait to label because you're saving up for a Cricut machine from Michaels (after which you'll also need to watch seven hours of YouTube videos to figure out how to put it together). A basic label maker costs less than $50, and you can pretty much label anything not made of fabric.

Here are some different label styles to consider, listed in order of general cost and complication level from least to greatest:

- **Label maker tape labels:** I recommend Brother brand
- **Printed labels:** I recommend Avery brand labels
- **Hand-lettered labels:** if you have dabbled in calligraphy or have super neat handwriting
- **Vinyl labels:** made with a Cricut or Silhouette machine; I recommend the Cricut Joy because it's smaller and easy to set up versus the big signature units.

What do you label? Anything and everything you can think to label. I know you assume you'll remember what's in those three baskets at the top of your closet, but I promise you that you will forget in seven to ten business days, so do your remaining brain cells a solid by creating a visual cue. It's one less thing you have to remember in the tasks you're continually tracking.

When it comes to a fabric bin at the top of a closet, there are a few ways to label. You can add a bin clip label and then print labels to insert. There are even some magnetic labels available now that can work with fabric; some may stay on better than others. Another option to consider is adding an inconspicuous label tape on the shelf below the bin. This can be done using black lettering on clear tape, which is subtly visible on the shelf surface. It is a discreet way to label and also super easy, because you can do so with any basic label maker.

Warning: in my mind the word "miscellaneous" is more offensive than the f-word. Don't you dare label anything in any space as "miscellaneous"! You might as well label it "hodge podge of shit I probably don't need." In my opinion, "miscellaneous" is a dirtier word than anything George Carlin ever said. (If you aren't sure who George Carlin is, it's worth a short laugh break on YouTube to find out.) Here's what I want you to do: hold up your right hand and repeat after me: "I, [insert name], do solemnly swear never to label anything in my home as 'miscellaneous.'" Find any other word to describe what is in your bin. Or if it really is that random, consider redistributing into other categories or finding a name that fits the majority of the contents.

When deciding what to label a certain category, it's best to be as specific as the space on the label allows. This is easier to do when using a label tape (letters are smaller and easy to change out) as opposed to a vinyl label (usually a two-word maximum due to size). Remember—the more specific the label, the better and the easier the flow of your life.

Just like a paint color can appear as different shades in different rooms, the ROAR process takes on new shapes in new spaces. Feel free to jump around to the spaces you are organizing or to download the knowledge first.

A NOTE ON TIMING AND SCOPE

Before you start this ROAR organizing process in spaces larger than a single drawer, you should be prepared for a few things. Everything takes longer than you anticipate. I have been organizing professionally for a decade, and organizing recreationally since I could read. Yet I can still overestimate my own solo accomplishment capability. Though I know a basic bathroom is a two-person, five- to six-hour job, my delusion is apparent when I think I can somehow knock out one of my own bathrooms in three to four hours. I have learned through many failed attempts to multiply my estimated project time by at least three.

Each project will take longer than you think, and you should allow a few to several days in a row to complete one space. It means taking into consideration that you may, at best, only have an hour or two available each day to dedicate to an organizing project, and you should also factor in the average adult attention span when our cell phones are buzzing every four seconds with notifications, texts, emails, and DMs. (If you can put your phone on Do Not Disturb for this hour of focused organizing, I would highly recommend it.) You should also overestimate your completion time needed and be kind to yourself when it takes even longer. That's why we schedule daily time to come back to it so you can keep the momentum going. It is crucial to set reasonable goals with a timeline that doesn't leave you feeling defeated.

Remember—we're breaking up each part of the process into chunks. Maybe each day is one letter of the ROAR process. This may mean your kitchen is a mess for a couple of days, but doing it thoughtfully and thoroughly is the long-term solution. Could you take off two weeks of work and send your family abroad in order to do it all at once? It would be nice, but there probably aren't many of us who have that kind of money and flexibility.

We also need to consider how life often comes at us and derails our plans—no one is immune to the bumps in the road, some of them even gaping potholes. It took me six months to design and organize my kids' playroom because I was determined to do it myself. That's right, six freaking months! Little chunks a couple of times a month were all I could dedicate. What I encourage you to do is continue through the process in ONE space all the way to labeling before starting a new space. This will ensure completion, which is what builds your organizing confidence and increases your momentum and excitement. When you can take a step back and admire a finished organization project, it can give you the push to keep going in more spaces.

A reminder that bears repeating: the mess gets worse before it gets better. The first step of our organizing process is removal—taking everything from the space so you can start fresh with a clean slate. Pulling out all the contents from a space, whether a closet or a kitchen or a bathroom, is absolutely overwhelming. It's the definition of a hot mess dumpster fire. All that stuff on the counters and tables or all that stuff taking over every surface in your bedroom is daunting.

Take a deep breath. This is why I'm reminding you again so that you are prepared for the jump scare. There is a purpose to the madness. Your ability to purge and decide what stays and what goes is best served with all the options in front of you. How can you know which workout outfits you want to keep until you have them all in front of you? Wouldn't it be easiest to decide on your favorite serving platters when you can see all of them together? This is the very reason we pull it all out—for full visibility, so you can make informed decisions.

Beware of the do-it-all domino effect. Sometimes you go to complete one task—let's say it's the area under your kids' sink—but you find yourself getting sucked into the vortex of overdoing it. Perhaps you find the shelf under your cabinet is wonky or slightly damaged from a previous water leak. You think, well, why should I do this space if I might redo this cabinet area? But if I'm gonna redo this cabinet area, I might as well do the floors below so I can do a floating vanity. Then before you know it, you're calling a contractor for an entire bathroom remodel. This is the do-it-all domino effect—what started as a modest organizing project under the sink suddenly escalated into a full-blown home construction project.

When we first bought our home, it was in its original early 1970s condition—lots of wallpaper and an abundance of wood paneling. Every space was showing its age, and I didn't want to spend a ton of money on a layout I knew wouldn't last long. The challenge was that I knew it needed to function and serve our family until we could set aside the budget for updating. Think about where to invest time and resources if you know you won't keep a space layout for the long haul.

In other words, don't buy the macramé basket to store your toilet paper if you anticipate a bathroom remodel in the next year or two. Instead, spend a couple of hours and a hundred bucks so your kids can get ready for school faster in the morning—worth the investment. A similar situation occurs when someone anticipates moving in the near future but wants to invest in their current home. It might make sense to do a large space like a closet that could add value to your home, but most people would rather forward their funds to a more long-term situation, which is understandable. When organizing a short-term solution under the pretense of future moving or renovation, you can reuse old products or even consider thrifting to keep the financial portion to a minimum.

USEFUL SUPPLIES TO HAVE BEFORE YOU BEGIN

- **Empty organizing containers.** Some of these may be discarded from other projects or left over from the last time you moved. Whatever you already own that's hanging around can prove useful, if even just to separate stuff into categories. We'll get to purchasing new products later, after we ROAR.

- **Sticky notes and a pen.** This is to temporarily label categories, which is also helpful when your project takes multiple days to complete.
- **Trash bin, recycle bin, donate bin.** These can be bags or actual bins; all that matters is you have one for each category you need. Sometimes you may need a "pass along" bin—your friend Bri would love these folding chairs you don't want since she hosts parties a lot, or the clothes your kids outgrow always go to your neighbor's younger son.
- **Label maker.** All my preferred products can be found on the LIKEtoKNOW.it app or Amazon, or you can use masking tape and a Sharpie and in the words of Tim Gunn from *Project Runway*, "Make it work!"
- **Stimulants and sanity.** If you run on pure adrenaline, I am in awe. Organizing is a physical job; treat it like you would a low-impact workout. If it's in the morning, you'll catch me with a cup of coffee. Sanity can be sourced through many forms—podcasts or your favorite upbeat tunes. Mine will always be any '90s alternative rock band, likely Incubus or Foo Fighters or the latest *SmartLess* podcast.

BREAD

ORGANIZING PRODUCT

Organizing products are the bins, baskets, and organizers used to perfect a newly sorted space. You can start by using what you have first, which is also kinder to your wallet. It is best to purchase any new organizing product after the ROAR process has been completed so that you're only shopping for the products you need as a completely informed, savvy, organized individual. After running point through the ROAR process, you will know EXACTLY what will be stored where. I share a lot of videos online to help you determine the best organizing product for your space. To get started on this step, you will need a measuring tape to measure the shelves or drawers or under-cabinet space you are trying to outfit and your smartphone to take photos and make notes. Obviously, you can start by trying out product you already own. The goal is to find product that fits the space well AND fits the category it is storing. For example, we wouldn't recommend fabric bins for your jams and jellies in the pantry; sticky and textile don't mix. If you're storing toys, slightly opaque boxes can be helpful for younger eyes. This process of choosing the right product for a specific space is what we in the biz call "sourcing." It can be tedious to analyze online product dimensions and compare them to your piles and shelf size, but I swear this is so much more efficient than guessing. It's like buying living room furniture: you need to know the size of your living room before choosing a couch size. If you take the time to do this part, you will save yourself many trips to the store or annoying returns to ship back.

Now that we've introduced you to the ROAR process, and hopefully you've had the chance to flex your organizing muscle on a mini space, let's get down to the nitty-gritty here on how this process changes shape in the different spaces of your home.

DON'T FORGET TO
DO GOOD + SHARE
SUCH SACRIFICES
PLEASE GOD

Chapter 6

EACH SPACE—STEP BY STEP

ORDER OF SPACES

The order you organize the spaces in your home matters. This is why I would never recommend you start with the garage or your primary wardrobe closet. It would be like deciding you wanted to learn how to cook and then beginning with a five-course French menu. Not a great place to begin or encouraging for a beginner chef. You develop organizing skills like you would any other skill or trade: with time and practice you'll grow and become more skilled. The order can vary for each person. One person's laundry room may be the easiest to start with, while someone else finds a bathroom a more controlled environment to tackle. You may decide that a single kitchen drawer at a time is where you're at, and that's okay too. Also note that the culprit may be hard to identify. When I hear someone tell me that their most disorganized space is their primary bedroom, I inquire about what categories they see in their bedroom. It's most often toiletries and clothes, and in fact, the culprit is a messy bathroom or closet (or both). Walk through your house and scribble down the least stressful space to the most stressful. You may have to flip through the remaining pages to follow your order, but I've done my best in the sections that follow to estimate a common pattern.

Homes and Vacation Homes

You've likely heard the phrase "everything needs a home" if you've read any organizing book or perused a cleaning blog. This means that everything you own needs to have an assigned spot or "home" in your home. I've learned over the last 10 years organizing professionally for hundreds of families that sometimes there is a permanent residence and a vacation home for one item. Shoes are a pretty common category with this kind of need. You have a few pairs of shoes needed by the exit or your back door (the vacation home) for quick escapes, but most live in your closet. We don't want everything to have two spots, but the few items that have seasons of high use

clothes
keys
+
wallet
slippers

followed by seasons of low use, such as winter gear or sports equipment, may need the option.

ENTRYWAY/MUDROOM

For some people, me included, the entryway/mudroom is one of the most difficult spaces to keep from looking as though our homes have been raided. Honestly, this area of my home more often looks like the aftermath of a ransacking rather than organized. In my family's defense, this room includes the door where we enter our home each day and shares duties with the laundry room and all utility and cleaning supplies. With barely a four-foot-wide section of wall and four people to support, including a stacked washer and dryer, it's no surprise this tight space is a constant challenge. Here are a few things I've learned along the journey of keeping this space under control.

I have to make use of every single inch of every wall. Seriously, the ceiling is the only place I haven't installed hooks or shelving.

I cannot buy in bulk. Sorry, Costco and Sam's Club groupies, but this may be a tough reality to face if the bulk is constantly in your way. If you live in a sizable space that can house 96 giant rolls of paper towels—hooray! You get those paper towels and 16 boxes of trash bags. For some of us (many of us? most of us?) it's an unreasonably large quantity to find room to store and truly a headache for most organizers to configure.

Finally, I've learned that this space has to be reassessed and tweaked often—every three months as the seasons and activities change. We are utilizing every available inch of space for storage, so I have to clean out, purge, and reconsider what's in there often, especially during the school year when the extracurricular activities are in overdrive. It's usually about the time I feel like I want to start lighting matches that I gruntingly force myself to address it, probably in the middle of a workweek when I'm fed up with tripping over shoes or laundry or sports bags for the 15th time in a row. Hence the channeling of that fed-up energy to promote change.

Hooks will be your best friend in any entry area or mudroom. They keep so much off the ground—hats, jackets, bags, umbrellas, leashes, you name it. Look for large coat hooks that can hold more weight and drill them in when possible, as that will be sturdier than a sticky strip. If it's not an option to drill, a 3M hook is better than nothing.

It's inevitable that a few shoes will find their way into the entryway/mudroom area and never leave. They multiply in my house like feral cats. Sure, it's a good idea to keep at least one pair of shoes per family member near the exit door for when you have to make a quick run to the mailbox or grocery store. Doing so takes away the hassle of trekking back to your closet just to escort the dog out to the lawn because he's so prissy and doesn't like getting his paws wet when it rains so you have to stand next to him with an umbrella while he pees. This is why my rain boots live at the back door.

Bags that frequently go in and out of the home may also make sense in this room if space allows. This also goes for briefcases, if you time-travel back to the 1960s and go by the name Don Draper. Another category should include school backpacks, gym bags, and hobby or sport bags. Depending on the sport, a backup option for storing these could be the garage. Having seen some of the equipment certain specialties require, I know some mudrooms may not have the space for all the hockey gear or softball catcher equipment. If these bags are too heavy for hooks or too bulky to hang on a shallow clearance wall, then a cubby, shelf, or basket is a great alternative. Wherever it goes, just make sure it has a home that isn't in the middle of the floor. Labeling will help the bag find its home again on most occasions, but as we know, the busyness of life may still lead it to a floor appearance. Try not to lose your cool on the offending bag abandoner, but rather kindly remind them of the home assigned for the bag—you know, the one labeled "Sal's Gym Bag."

No matter the size of your house, most mudrooms are limited, which means you have to be critical about the items and categories that legitimately need to be stored here. These should be things frequently needed, as in multiple times a week. A test for the mudroom space might be to clear out most of your possessions and shoes and stuff and then see what comes back and accumulates over the next month. This will give the best clarity on what needs a long-term home in your entry mudroom space.

LAUNDRY/UTILITY ROOM

Oy vey—this is a tough room for instituting any order. Talk about an evolving room of chaos. From batteries to cleaning supplies to bug spray to laundry detergent, this room holds a lot of random stuff. If you're lucky, yours came equipped with ample storage. If you're not so lucky, you may need to add some. You should aim to fill the largest wall with top-to-bottom storage. I've come across very few laundry/utility rooms with storage space to spare, which means we have to improvise with the available space. Maximize what you have, and if your budget allows, consider revamping with a new layout. My teeny-tiny laundry space also moonlights as the mudroom, so we have less than six feet of space to store a washer, a dryer, and all our cleaning and washing supplies—plus hang backpacks, store workout and activity bags, and stash the run-out-to-the-mailbox or the hurry-up-we're-late-for-school sneakers. This pocket of my home is a constant organizing challenge. I have to remind the other people in my house (**cough** my kids **cough**) that this room is not a dumping ground and must remain a pass-through. And one day my kids will hang their backpacks without me asking them to, right? If you're also

toilet
napkin
towel
dog
LG

working in tight quarters, keep your product quantities small and manageable.

In true form, counters (or any flat surface for that matter) are magnets for stuff—and if it isn't managed over time, this stuff becomes clutter, as if horizontal surfaces were a vortex sucking in anything nearby. Why? The item doesn't have a home, or we don't take the time to put it in its home (in my house it's the latter).

Our mudroom/laundry/utility room is the messiest space in my house most days, the most used, and the one that needs tweaking the most often. Laundry is an ongoing task in most households, and even more so when there are small humans who can't take care of their own laundry needs yet. This means extra chores for parents, and let's face it: we could barely manage our own dirty clothes before the little gremlins came along.

Leaving out the items traditionally associated with the mudroom (since we addressed that topic earlier), most laundry rooms will include the following categories:

- **Detergent/laundry soap**
- **Stain removers**
- **Scent agents** (like Unstoppables or scented dryer sheets)
- **Cleaning supplies**
- **Laundry baskets**

- **Pet supplies.** In our home, we have a special needs canine who has three different types of diapers and also needs changing at least twice a day. This takes up a pretty large amount of space, but your pet category may only have food, bowls, leashes, treats, and animal meds.
- **Paper goods.** Napkins, toilet paper, facial tissue, paper towels, and the like. Not everyone will have this category in their laundry rooms, but many do since these items are used by everyone in the household, so it's helpful to have one restocking zone.

Analyzing this area may be easier than most—you either use it or you don't. The Return portion of ROAR is even more tricky if you're very limited on space. This may mean you only have room for a six-pack of paper towels and one laundry station refill. Don't be tempted to undo a system just because Target is offering a $10 gift card if you buy three or more; I've made that mistake, and those two extras sat on a flat surface for two months. As you return items to their new homes, consider whether a "station set" near your washer is needed (with the rest of the restock items stored in another area). We talked about this in terms of your bathroom sink area as well: you keep your current set of skincare handy, and refills have another spot. Storing like with like isn't a hard-and-fast rule all the time but should allow flexibility for busy lifestyles.

ESCAPE THE
ORDINARY

HOME OFFICE OR STUDY

Here's a space that certainly had a moment in 2020. If you didn't already have a designated area and were lucky enough to have a job that could be done from a computer at home, then you were in a hot hurry to set up a home office after COVID shut the world and most cubicle offices down. My home serves as the Organized Life Design headquarters. When I say I'm in the office, in reality that space is our former dining room transformed. Our actual dining room used to be the formal sitting room back in the 1970s when this was a thing, but who needs one of those anymore in this day and age? The home office sometimes isn't a whole room but a portion of a room shared with another space. We commonly see home offices that are also guest rooms or another multipurpose room like a crafting space. During the pandemic when all we "nonessentials" were forced to work from home—or in our case, filing for unemployment since we were neither essential nor could we organize our clients' homes from afar—a surge of creating efficient home offices with Zoom-call-appropriate background walls became essential.

There is certainly a balance to strike between a productive and aesthetically pleasing office. It begins by removing #allthethings from your drawers, cabinets, desks, and boxes. Next, everything should be organized into the following categories:

- **Writing tools.** This category includes pens, pencils, and markers.
- **Books.** The ones related to your career or craft, or to impress the people who see you on a virtual call.
- **Office supplies.** All the Post-its, glue, paper clips, binder clips, tape, tape dispensers, Wite-Out (shout-out to all of us perfectionists out there), staples, staplers, and the like go here.
- **Printer.** If you're Gen Z I'm guessing you skip this category, which includes any ink cartridges and different types of printing paper—photo, cardstock, and regular-ass printing paper.
- **Mailing supplies.** Envelopes, packaging, tape, and stamps are in this grouping.
- **Labels.** Most pro organizers boast an impressive array of printable label sizes, and perhaps you do too.
- **Paper.** *Oy vey*, paper is a bitch. There's no other way to say it. Paper is such a bore, and no matter how many times you go through it, more always appears. We'll deep-dive into paper in the next section.
- **Occasional cards.** All the happy birthday, wedding, new home, and get well cards are here so you can, you know, use them.
- **Electronics.** This category is generally small devices like cameras, e-readers, and hopefully label makers. It could also include scanners and tablets.

- **Cords and cables.** This category is a real see-you-next-Tuesday, if you catch my drift. The constant evolution of electronics leads us to acquire multiple cords and cables in every configuration possible for every device ever owned. It drives me bananas. B-A-N-A-N-A-S. Occasionally we get rid of the old devices, but the cables stick around like an unwanted pest problem. Best Buy is the largest electronic device recycler I know of that also accepts cords and cables. Set aside a bag to drop off on your next errand rotation.

As you are analyzing these groups, I want you to be extra critical of paper and cords and cables, as these are some of the fastest-growing groups as well as the hardest to keep under control.

After the initial shock of the pandemic subsided in 2021 and folks were comfortable having strangers come into their homes again, home offices and studies were among the most popular spaces we organized throughout 2022. A lot had changed as far as layout needs in a home office—having a video-call-appropriate backdrop became imperative, so those working at home could at least resemble people who have their shit together. When possible, floating your desk is better than putting it against a wall, because it has better visibility and lighting from every direction. If you face a window, it's even better for your complexion on screen and you can also minimize glare on a computer screen and have direct light on your face. Who doesn't want to appear fresh-faced on those group calls when you're actually wearing pajamas? (As long as you're not the lawyer who looks like a cat, you're fine; this is the moment when I would pull out my phone and show you the video from 2020 on YouTube that made me laugh until I cried.)

Organizing your office supplies is important, but what I find to be the first priority is the layout, because it influences function and determines what storage furniture is needed next. The layout of your office depends on a few variables. You may be asking yourself what type of desk you should get. If you do have a desk floating in the room, it is best to choose something less bulky like a writing desk, which basically looks like a table with one or two writing utensil drawers. If the back of the desk is visible, that's something to consider when choosing. To maintain the room's flow, a bulky bottom file drawer is not ideal when a desk is positioned in the middle of a space.

Unless you're an accountant or a lawyer, most of us aren't accessing several paper files a day. If you do use some paper and need a few files, you can try a desktop file sorter or a single file drawer, which is best against a wall or incorporated into a bookcase. As far as other storage needs are concerned in a home office, if the room has a closet, that's a good place to start. Many home offices are extra bedrooms or guest rooms, either converted or doing double duty. Utilize the closet area efficiently before adding any other storage in the room. An old nightstand can be used as storage for small office supplies like writing tools, notepads, and paper clips. Stacking plastic drawers can also do the trick. When you have paper files to store that don't need to be accessed frequently, they can be kept in a file drawer tucked away in the closet.

If you've maxed out the available closet space or if you didn't have one to begin with, then you can consider additional storage furniture around your desk area. Most common is book storage, and I've seen every size collection from a handful of business titles to a collection worthy of being called Belle's *Beauty & the Beast* library. My personal book collection falls into the latter category because ya girl has been a bookworm since the third grade. You'd be hard-pressed to tear my hard copy books away from me. There may have been another organizing book previously published that recommended donating books you have already read, but as someone who has read several titles more than once or refers back to books I've read, this is advice I will not endorse. When I read a *meh* novel I've been known to pass it along, but this is the extent of my ability to let go of books. And I won't apologize for it.

It bears repeating: as long as you can store the quantity of items you wish to store in your home and they fit, then by all means keep all you want. Books can be clutter if they are overwhelming a space and don't have a home shelf to live on, but they can also be part of a cherished collection of interests and memories. Your physical limitation is the space you designate for books, so you can fill to the brim, my friend! (If I were Belle, this is where the music montage in the village would begin, where everyone makes fun of me for reading.)

All right: let's get back to storage furniture. In addition to book storage, you may need storage for office supplies, mailing supplies, folders, binders, and perhaps a printer. I love converting a buffet table or a bookcase with an enclosed cabinet on the bottom for storing these items. Seeing all your categories and how much you need to store can help you determine the right size of storage furniture needed.

Client spotlight: one dude, let's call him Simon, had a home office that also served as his hobby space. He loved to build model planes and take apart old radios. A lot of storage furniture was needed, as well as compartments for all the tiny little things his hobby created. We repositioned his desk so the backdrop on his work video calls was not his current in-progress plane, but rather a bookcase displaying the finished ones.

Now, let's dive deeper into paper. I can hear you sigh and possibly panic at the daunting task of tackling the paper in your house. Honey, I've been there—actually I'm there right now, again, for the zillionth time. Cue melting face emoji. Paper finds its way into my house as easily as dust. We can set up systems for processing it, but it truly never fails—at least once a year I need a complete overhaul, and monthly some tweaking to keep it at bay.

Second to maybe food, it's probably the quickest category to multiply.

That "touch once" rule is dumb. If you've never heard it before, it's a rule that recommends only touching a piece of paper once and taking the action needed immediately. It has been made popular by many organizers. Good on you if this is something you've mastered. I have yet to meet someone who was able to actually follow this rule for longer than a week. It's dumb because it's impossible to achieve for overworked, exhausted adults in 2024. When organizers tout it as the standard, it sets people up for failure because they become so discouraged by the insurmountable maintenance of this system that they quickly give up. It falls in the same category as the zero email inbox rule, which I also think is outdated to today's average person trying to adult; it sets an impossible standard.

There's no shortage of cute boxes that can be used for storage in these home office and study spaces—just be sure to keep them as clearly labeled as possible. Magazine boxes are awesome for storing empty folders, envelopes, mailing supplies, notepads, trade magazines, and anything that would save you space by being vertical as opposed to lying around in piles of confusion. After you determine the right storage solution, purchased or maybe even built, you can start moving into that bad boy. Keep the things you need access to most often at the easiest-to-reach spots, and the rest can go below or behind.

My prayer is that you take what you need from this book and apply what works to your life. If one of these suggestions doesn't suit your lifestyle, then feel free to give it the middle finger. You won't hurt my feelings—but you will if you try something, learn it doesn't work for you, and then conclude you are a failure who will never be organized. THAT would hurt my heart!

Tackling the Paper

I'm gonna give it to you straight. Organizing paper sucks balls. It's not fun for anyone. Never has there ever been one person on my team who has walked away from a paper organizing project for a client and said, "Man, that was a bitchin' good time!" Not a single one. After all, paper projects move like molasses (and if that's not a saying where you live, then try this one: it's as slow as watching paint dry).

Going through stacks of paper is slow and tedious and requires a lot of reading. To be honest, organizing rarely requires any reading unless it's an expiration date on a can of tomatoes. That's one of the appeals to me: it's an on-your-feet activity with very little sitting still. (Well, I guess in this instance you're sitting still because you're reading this book, but let's call it research. I digress.)

Tackling your papers needs to be approached with patience and a lot of bribing. Seriously, treat yourself like a kid who doesn't want to do their homework or a toddler who doesn't want to eat their dinner—how can you bribe

yourself into undertaking this part of the process? What I will tempt you with is the satisfying feel-like-a-badass-who's-got-their-shit-together feeling that comes after handling and filing away important documents. If upgrading your sunglasses via the Nordstrom cart is also a carrot to dangle, then you do you. Don't forget to retire an old pair of sunglasses—remember, one in, one out.

Organizing paperwork will save you money in the long run. It might be money in terms of the time you save when you know exactly where the title to the car you sold is located rather than spending hours ripping apart your house or having to order another one, which costs actual money and time. In prep for your date with organizing, gather file folders, pen or label maker, if you have the capacity, and that ominous stack of who-the-hell-knows-what. Here's a trick on file folders that runs counter to the way most sets are sold: use folders with tabs on the same side. It looks more organized than left, middle, and right, which gets jacked up when you add new files. Anyway, I prefer mine all right-tabbed.

You may also consider a large size of your go-to treat beverage and some upbeat tunes. I enjoy wearing headphones when I organize in my home because it keeps me focused—music, a podcast, or Audible are all great choices. Streaming a TV show can end up being a distraction unless it's your tenth round of *Gilmore Girls*. Save the latest gnarly reality dating show for clothes-folding time. It's too compelling to judge these peoples' terrible love interests to be distracted by an organizing project; when you do a mindless towel-folding sesh, you can really dig into the spectacle.

Now, back to paper organizing. You've got your supplies and your motivation; now it's time to rock 'n' roll. Keep your categories super-duper easy-peasy—like "Medical 2024." Unless you have ongoing medical conditions that require several appointments a month, no need to categorize by doctor or field of medicine. You can separate by person in the household if needed, but I always recommend the fewest categories possible when it comes to paper filing.

The same goes for banking, household services, taxes, cars—again, keep it as general as you can considering we rarely pull these files out, often only in need of reference. Your cars file may include a title for each vehicle or maybe a purchase record and major maintenance records, but that's about it. If you bring your car to the same place for maintenance, they may send you these documents via email and keep records in their electronic system, so storing a third paper copy in your home may be redundant for something you'll never refer to on paper again. This isn't 1999. The buyer will want your VIN and maybe the last time you purchased tires. Supplying a paper copy for every oil change doesn't do much but create a filing headache for you—not to mention the space for file cabinets that could be used for something else.

If you are employed by someone else, you need one file with the name of your company, and you can stick what you need in there. However, if you do your own thing, like work as a 1099 contractor or run your own small business, then it would be beneficial to break the needed categories up. As my business has grown, so have my file categories, but I prefer to file digitally as much as possible (we'll get to that in a minute). Think marketing, expenses, subcontractors, financials—broad subjects. Banking could be yearly statements for each bank, and depending on your financial portfolio (one of those business school words that just means how many different places you keep your cash money, honey), you may divvy up by investments accounts, property, and so on.

Household services should only include major projects—the bathroom renovation, paint colors, and the receipt for the new water heater (if not digitized when purchased). Do you have to keep the manual for the thermostat? If you don't know how to use one or can't figure out how to google a copy of the manual, then we might have bigger fish to fry than getting organized. Every receipt for each air filter is not a recommended keep item either.

Taxes can be copies of your returns. Check irs.gov for most updated recommendations on how long to keep your tax returns. As of the printing of this book, if you do not have multiple sources of income, you only need to keep five years of returns, not including the current unfiled year. If you do have multiple streams of income because you work as a contractor, meaning a previous employer could come back and suddenly add $10,000 to your earned wages six years later, then the IRS recommends keeping seven years of tax filing records, not including the present year in which you are still earning money.

Once upon a time decades ago, I would keep all the utility bills I was ever sent. I even wrote down the date I submitted payment or mailed the check. Yes, young Earthling, this was how we did it 20-plus years ago. These days, I don't even receive my utility bills in the mail. Sign up for paperless billing for everything you possibly can. It will minimize a chunk of the paper that comes into your house. If you feel comfortable about it, set up automatic payments for those bills as well. If it's for a credit card, set up auto for the minimum, then just check in a couple of times a month to pay off all or what you can over the minimum. Paperless billing and automatic minimum payments are intended to make your life easier to manage, which is the whole point.

Let's Talk Digital Filing

Let's get digital, dig-it-al. (Get it? It rhymes with "physical," like we're back in 1981 listening to Olivia Newton-John on the radio.) Don't be scared! I'll start by saying this isn't for everyone; there are some people (**cough** boomers **cough**) who will insist on keeping all the paper copies, and you know what, I don't argue. You do you, boo. We may need a few more filing drawers than the average household. As for those interested in the concept, there is almost

always a bit of a hybrid. Keep the major stuff but digitize as much as you can.

Start today. What paper did you encounter today that you would like to keep as a record? Perhaps a UPS confirmation of a package, because it's a temporary reference. As soon as the store confirms the return, that white slip of paper is trash. On the other hand, you could snap a photo of it immediately upon receiving it in your hand and toss it as you walk out of the customer service department.

Rather than tell you to go back to digital filing your pay stubs starting from 2004, first I'm going to tell you to chunk it, because the IRS will not come after you for a tax return older than seven years. So whatever year you're reading this—maybe 2025, so minus seven years is 2017, meaning anything before that is gone-zo—shred them yourself or take them to your local pack-and-ship store to securely shred them for a small fee. Yes, you might pay $80 for a couple of boxes, but I promise, your small office shredder wasn't meant to do large-scale shred sessions, and the way they make electronic equipment these days, you're more likely to burn out the motor or grind down the teeth. Those shredders were meant for the occasional expired credit card, not 12 years of unsorted paperwork.

When creating a new digital paper management system, start with what you need to address today (whatever you want to keep a paper copy of) and take a photo of it. The easiest way to do this is to snap a photo with your phone and tag it as "favorite"—that little heart icon that pulls up in your phone photos. If you want to generate a digital system and sort one step further, create a paperwork folder on your phone photos and title it by year. I want this to be so easy that you feel silly when trying to make excuses not to do it. Now if you're really feeling randy about digital paper organizing, I encourage you to use an app to store these documents. Evernote is my preferred choice, but it does require a monthly fee. The bonus is that I can save any photos I take with my phone as a PDF or jpg, and I can access these files from another device. Other options are Scanner app and OneNote. I'm sure there are dozens more, but who can possibly keep up with them all? It's important to label the folders you're saving these digital files to with the simplest of names—Medical 2024, Home Services 2024, or School Year 2025–26—something easily recognizable and quick to recall.

So what should you keep on paper? The answer is simple—as little as possible. I have an "In-Process" letter organizer on my desk for projects that are active or items I need to refer to regularly. It becomes a hot mess about once a month, which is my visual reminder to go back through and reorganize. I have one file cabinet in our house for the titles, closing docs, and other similar documents that are best to have paper copies of on hand. Last, I have one small, easy-access file sorter in my office that serves those in-between needs—current active house project not ready to retire to the long-term storage file cabinet or not yet ready to digitize because they're incomplete. Again, paper is an evolving system because you, my friend, are an evolving human. As there is no such thing as one-size-fits-all clothes, there is no one-size paper organizing file system that fits all people. Treat your paper system like a mythical phoenix: once in a while it'll burst into metaphorical flames and you'll have to start all over.

While I despise the term "dream job," which somehow implies a scenario that doesn't feel like working, I do believe we should enjoy the kind of work we do—maybe not every second of every day, but a majority of the time. A huge impactful part of enjoying our work is the environment in which we do it. Whether you work from home all the time or only occasionally, your office space should be an inviting and happy space. Don't forget to add personal touches like artwork and pops of color if that's your jam. A fun rug and your favorite slippers are also brilliant additions for a home office. When you don't have clutter screaming at you the second you walk into your office, the more likely you are to stay focused and power through your workday.

LIVING ROOM

In my house, particularly during hectic work and school weeks, you can find an impressive mountain range of laundry piles separated and half folded covering no less than half of the seating area. There will also be an assortment of toys,

books, shoes, and art supplies sprinkled over the floor like oversized confetti. Do we shift, shuffle, and fold the same piles of laundry until we're fed up enough to put them all away? Sure. (Also, "Shift, Shuffle, and Fold" sounds like a great 1950s rock 'n' roll song—where's Little Richard on the piano when you need him?!)

This is what a busy life looks like with kids and two parents working outside the home. The same parents are exhausted on the weekends and don't have the patience to micromanage their tiny humans for a cleaning spree. I've advocated several times for my family to become nudists and eliminate laundry altogether, but it hasn't been met with much enthusiasm. Most of what clutters living rooms doesn't even live there. In my case, all the clothes belong in closets, toys and books should be in the kids' rooms, and shoes should live in their assigned spots but seem to wander to the living room like there's a secret shoe magnet. The living room may be an easier room to clear out initially since much doesn't belong here; however, it has a domino effect on needing to address other spaces.

"Store it where you use it" is one of my favorite professional organizer rules to apply while clearing out a living room. You may find there are some categories that need a home in this central space. Perhaps board games are played on the coffee table, or maybe your dog supplies could be usefully stored next to the kennels in the family room. These are the considerations when you find the same categories congregating frequently in the same space. Perhaps your embroidery set should find a permanent spot next to your comfy recliner since that is your favorite place to create, rather than in the upstairs guest closet, where it never seems to end up anyway. When deciding where to store something, ask yourself: Where do I use this most often? That's where it should be stored.

Furniture can play a dual role in living rooms: think coffee tables with storage drawers or bookcases with enclosed bottom cabinets. These can serve an organizational function as well as being a cozy place to host friends for game night or cousins for movie night. Again, move the categories that don't belong in the living area somewhere else, but be flexible when something needs to find a permanent residence or a "vacation home," as mentioned earlier.

KITCHEN

Hot diggity dog, let's organize the kitchen, ladies and gentlemen! The kitchen is one of the most used spaces, and this is what makes it one of the most impactful places in the home to organize. We gather here and then we eat, then we eat again, and later on, dang it, do we need to eat again? Those of us who eat most meals at home and often cook their own meals will see the result of a messy kitchen every single day. And by "cook often" I mean anything from full-on from-scratch meals to heating up leftovers. With all my dietary restrictions, eating at home is safest for me. If you're one of those meal planners who makes weekly trips to the grocery store, then you have a kitchen disaster to deal with weekly as well.

Fear not: having a mess to deal with doesn't mean you're disorganized. That stuff on your counter isn't clutter when you're able to clean up the kitchen and return everything to its assigned home. If gadgets, dishes, or appliances must be kept on counters because there isn't a home to return them to, then, my darling, we may have to accept the stuff-on-the-counter look.

It's important to analyze what stays on our counter and whether that's the vacation home to a more permanent location for the item in question. Take my blender and toaster, for example: they're not daily-use items for me and have a corner cabinet spot, but are often found on my counter due to laziness or . . . well, laziness. I used to frequent Sur La Table, which I recently learned means "on top of the table" (thanks Duolingo French), so I'm familiar with the kitchen-gadget-acquiring temptation. What I have realized is that having only six drawers total in the kitchen for #allthethings, it's pretty cutthroat when it comes to determining which food tools deserve a place. For every tool or gadget you consider buying, ask yourself: Can the same task be done with a knife? Or with some other currently owned gadget? It's the Hunger Games in my drawers: we've had eight years in this space and there's no more room to grow, so one of these gadgets has to volunteer as tribute for another to move in. "One in, one out" exists in my kitchen, especially with food storage containers. With a chef-worthy knife collection, there are few new fad gadgets that could do the job better.

Just as with the bathroom, I don't believe in zero items on the counter in the kitchen either. If you make smoothies every single day, maybe keeping the blender or a nutribullet on the countertop makes your life run more smoothly (ha, see what I did there, smoothly and smoothies). I keep my smoothie ingredients on the counter in the corner along with my dry ingredients, in cutely labeled containers, of course, but they stay on the counter for ease and simplicity in my daily routine. Remember, everything we do in terms of designing your organized life involves understanding the habits you lean into, which determines the setup that suits your lifestyle. Another way I lean in to my lifestyle is when it comes to having a dish-drying rack next to the sink 24/7. Considering I live in a fast-paced world with a family, in a humid environment where the dishwasher dryer is about as useful as a box of hair, means that I constantly—as constantly as I am breathing—have wet dishes that need to air out. Could I use a dish towel to absorb all that moisture and place the dishes back in their rightful home? Maybe, but I don't want to or maybe it's one of those oddly shaped kitchen items with crevices and I don't have the patience to figure out how to dry it short of pulling out a hair dryer.

That seems excessive, although the thought does delight my OCD senses.

Categories that find themselves in harmony in the kitchen include:

- **Dishes.** Duh . . . this includes your plates, snack plates, dinner plates, bowls, pasta bowls, cereal bowls—well, you get the idea.
- **Drinking vessels.** This breaks down into all your cups, glasses, mugs, and water bottles. If you have a designated area for barware, keep it separate from your daily drinking vessels.
- **Appliances.** Your microwave is likely staying put, but appliances include things like food processors, blenders, toasters, slow cookers, instant pots, air fryers, rice cookers, smoothie makers, egg cookers, waffle makers, and if you are a fancy bitch raised in the '80s or '90s, your panini presses. We can further divide this category into frequently used small appliances and the other shit you paid too much money to get rid of yet will find room to store somewhere high up until you forget about it or one day when you move you find it in that cabinet above the fridge and think oh, this is where the ice cream maker has been the whole time!
- **Food storage containers.** For my elder millennials, Gen Xers, and boomers, we call this Tupperware regardless of the actual brand label. (Like Kleenex, which is not the name of the facial tissue product you

blow your nose with but rather the most commonly used brand that we now refer to as a noun even if it's actually a brand.) I'm gonna grill you on what to keep in this self-multiplying category in a hot second.

- **Cookware.** These consist of your pots, pans, and associated lids as well as baking dishes (in the way your recipes refer to as 8x8, 9x13), and their friends.
- **Baking tools.** These can run the gamut depending on whether you're the occasional baker who churns out a box of muffins once a month or my baby daddy, who can make the most delicious gluten-free, dairy-free scones from scratch. This will also include measuring cups, spoons, mixing bowls, biscuit cutters, icing tips, and so on.
- **Flatware.** Also known as "silverware," whether it's actually silver or not. (Most of these items today are in fact stainless steel and are technically termed "flatware.") Or whatever you wanna call the pokey tool you use to shove food in your face hole.
- **Kids' dishes.** These are best kept separate and more accessible than your regular dinnerware if space allows, if your kids are the age requiring their own dishware. As an ever-evolving category depending on how old your little goblins happen to be, you should constantly reevaluate what can be retired and whether that freebie cup from the last restaurant is dishwasher safe and BPA-free.

- **Large, flat things.** Cutting boards, cookie sheets, pizza stones, and other large, flat things that get clumped together. These generally require storage space accommodations, which is why they are best brought together in their own category.
- **Knives.** Probably the most useful multiuse tool in your kitchen. Investing in an excellent chef's knife and paring knife will serve you for years and maybe even decades—not to mention being a better option for many tasks than some fancy gadget, as noted earlier.

A typical American kitchen takes a team of three organizers one full day to whip into shape. Consider the average size to be a room with two eight-foot-wide walls with an assortment of cabinets and drawers, then add an island, add a person. Breaking down each part of your kitchen may be a more manageable task to tackle on your own, but it may be a project that takes up kitchen and dining tables for a couple of days while you reunite the categories you've sorted out.

These larger spaces can be most challenging when tackling solo. You might feel like you're on a treasure hunt pulling together all the like items. Find all the coffee cups. Put all the small appliances together. Worst of all are the food storage containers. Here's where I do the grilling part when it comes to food storage containers—no lid, no stay. It's kind of like no shoes, no service: you either have shoes and can go in the establishment, or if you wander in toes out and feet bare, you'll be asked to leave. We're going to apply the same rule to our Tupperware (**ahem**) food storage containers—if it doesn't have a lid, it needs to be discarded. To determine how many food storage containers you need to keep, take a look at what your fridge is holding at this moment. Maybe you use two or three for leftovers or maybe you and your partner meal plan for the week, so you need to have 10 for quick, easy lunches. Either way, whatever you're regularly using plus three to four as backups is really all you need to own. You run your dishwasher at least once a week, right? In my house that thing runs at least every other day.

Physical space can be your purge detector for any kitchen category. If the cabinet you have for storing all the food storage containers can fit everything you have, bravo! All can stay. However, if it's exploding and you have way more than you can feasibly store, time to pick favorites in food storage containers. I recommend that glass containers get first dibs because of longevity (as long as they have lids).

Do your best to avoid two places to store the same category in the kitchen. This is where the brushfire of clutter begins, and you're likely to reach for one area over and over while the second area is forgotten. Keep this in mind for cups, which is one of the fastest categories to become overwhelming in any kitchen. (Yes, I am side-eyeing your Stanley collection and lookin' at myself and my coffee cup menagerie in this instance.)

We eat most of our meals at home, which means for at

least breakfast and dinner each day we're producing a pile of dishes. This creates a lot of micromanaging and makes it hard to keep the kitchen clean and under control. It's also next to our tiny laundry mudroom, which means it absorbs the spillover of school papers and activity bags and therefore is a constant mess most days during the week. Extend grace to yourself and remember: we're only aiming for *passing* here, and no one will be named valedictorian.

PANTRY

Heaven's bells on a sunny day, do I love me a pantry project! My pantry is the most popular and nationally published of any of my personal spaces, thank you very much (cue that emoji with the hand primping hair on one side or the one with the blushed cheeks that could be whistling or making a kissy face, I'm not sure). My pantry was a passion project with no rules for color, so I brought in bright lemon motif wallpaper and retro pink appliances, and I have no regrets. As much as I adore a chic organizing layout with rainbow-ordered clear bins, it didn't suit my style, nor the tornado children who would not keep it arranged that way for long.

Everyone eats—which is why food organization applies to all. And the pantry is the space needing the most frequent attention, because most of us go to the grocery store at least once a week. If you're a European, *bonjour*: you're probably wondering why the heck we Americans need a small grocery

FLOUR
gf flour
spreads
cans
bags & wrap
chips & popcorn
nuts
snacks
udi's
dinner
kid snacks

SMEG
SMEG
pasta
light brown sugar
dark brown sugar
gf flour
FLOUR
SANTA CRUZ
cans
Justin's

store in our fat kitchens when you generally have a cupboard and swing by the market almost daily. My response is the emoji with shrug arms to each side and a quizzical face. Not only do we make frequent trips to the store, but we also stock up like an apocalypse is right around the corner. I'm not a huge fan of stockpiling because food spoils, and where the heck are we supposed to fit a barrel of tomato sauce and how would this even feed us when the zombies come?

The different cultures and ethnicities here in Houston make it a fun and interesting place to work inside people's homes. We see all types of foods and cuisines in our clients' pantries. Feel free to personalize your pantry to fit your cooking style and manage an appropriate flow for your everyday needs. These are the most common categories we find in the pantry food storage areas:

- **Grains**
- **Pastas**
- **Dinner.** I love using this general category to assign to a fluid group of "What's for dinner?" One week it might be mac and cheese, and the next it might be specific ingredients for a recipe you're making. In my case it always includes taco seasoning and taco shells. My Mexican-ness also shows up in my pantry in the assortment of different beans I keep on hand.
- **Chips, popcorn, and pretzels.** If you have the space to separate these, do it!

- **Crackers**
- **Breakfast**
- **Cereal**
- **Smoothie ingredients.** It can also be called "Protein and pre-workout," if that suits you better.
- **Candy and sweets**
- **Chocolate.** If this doesn't fit into other sweets and it needs its own category in your kitchen, no shade.
- **Baking ingredients.** This encompasses your baking soda, baking powder, cornstarch, Crisco for us Southern folk, and can also include sprinkles, icing, muffin/cupcake liners, and other baking accoutrements.
- **Medicine.** Many meds and supplements need to be taken with food and water, which means it makes sense to keep them in the same place as the food. For the sake of convenience, this often makes sense for the time of day when medicines and supplements are taken—morning or evening—and can include daily vitamins as well as your family's entire personal pharmacy. (If the pantry doesn't work for this category for you, another option is a kitchen cabinet in a handy location.)
- **Small appliances.** Meaning the ones that don't fit in the kitchen. In most setups, these include the rice cookers and instant pots that may only make a once-a-month appearance. If you're super extra like me, you may have a few pink appliances primarily for aesthetic

reasons that also count as backups if our blender or mixer breaks—and living on the top shelf of our pantry where they can be admired when they're not being used is the perfect home for them.

- **Disposable paper products.** Your plastic cutlery, paper plates, and Solo cups that make an appearance for parties or large gatherings need one spot to live. I pretend I'm saving the planet by using biodegradable versions. If you have space, you can divide these into multiple bins and label each accordingly.
- **Paper goods.** This includes paper towels and napkins, unless they live in a utility area instead of your pantry.

Unlike a guest room, the pantry is a space accessed multiple times a day by possibly every human in your home. As dietary needs and snack preferences change, you'll need to tweak the pantry often to keep it maintained. The pantry is one of the highest values in terms of return on investment. Maintaining an organized pantry helps you waste less food, because you can find what you need when you need it, and save money because you don't overbuy. Most of us go grocery shopping at least once a week, so incoming products mean you have to find room for everything to be put away.

Pantries might tie with closets for the most popular spaces we organize, and honestly it's my favorite—shhh . . . don't tell closet! There aren't as many emotions involved in pantries as with closets—no one is having feelings of shame over the chips that expired like they might with a pair of pants they haven't fit in for years. I've been there personally. It's almost always a faster turnaround than a closet as well, which means the fun part of admiring your hard work comes sooner. Everyone eats and buys food, so this makes it an impactful space to reset.

Product recommendations in the pantry depend on your budget, as well as the look you are creating. I generally steer away from fabric because of how easily it stains, and avoid flimsy bins that can't handle being constantly pulled off the shelf. Everything from wood bins to woven baskets can work in this space, and I encourage you to play with texture here.

CLOSETS

Buckle up, *amigas*, because this space is a doozy. Reload your water bottle, top off your iced tea, grab a snack, and roll up your sleeves. Why are closets one of the most difficult spaces to organize? Closets hold a lot of emotional baggage for any human who has dealt with health issues or weight fluctuations. We all have self-image issues and shopping addictions (spoken as a recovering anorexic with body dysmorphia, topped off with an anxiety-fueled add-to-cart problem). I'm on a first-name basis with UPS, FedEx, and USPS. Feelings of self-worth, guilt, shame, and depression can all reveal themselves in what accumulates in our closets.

winter
sun
art
Oscar de la Renta
Christian Louboutin
swim

Like I warned you, this category is a doozy. Be patient AND kind to yourself during this process.

Closets are one of those spaces where the purging and decluttering part of the process is one of the most time-consuming portions of the process. We lean hard into the "Remove" part of ROAR here. In a pantry or kitchen, it's either expired or you don't use it; the end. (Do you use an avocado slicer? No? Okay, chuck it.) When it comes to clothes, we're in an entirely different ballpark. We're not even playing the same sport. Does it fit? Yes. Do you wear it? No. So get rid of it? Maybe? If it fits our body—or even if it used to fit and doesn't right now—we attach usefulness to it, even if we don't love the color or the style.

But even if we can fit something on our bodies, that doesn't deem it useful enough to earn a place in your closet. More important than whether it is the right size, we should consider the following: How do we feel when we wear it? Do we know how to style it or what to wear with it? Is it comfortable? There are so many more variables to consider. You should know going into this space that you won't finish in a day—heck, I'll be impressed if you do it all in a week. Pace yourself, and don't be discouraged if it takes a couple of weeks to reach that finally done feeling.

Let's categorize the closet:

- **Tops.** Shirts, blouses, T-shirts, and any item of your wardrobe addressing the area of your body between your neck and your belly button. Feel free to separate further by sleeve length.

- **Bottoms.** Pants, shorts, skirts, and anything made to cover your ass in public.
- **Dresses**
- **Shoes**
- **PJs or pajamas or nightwear**
- **Athleisure.** Your workout clothes and #allthethings in which you break a sweat.
- **Underwear and undergarments**
- **Bras.** For those of you with boobs.
- **Socks.** For those of you with feet.
- **Fashion accessories.** This includes belts, hats, jewelry, handbags, and the like. Separate further as needed.

Okay, we divided #allthethings. Now comes the real struggle with the analysis portion of your wardrobe. There are three fun ways to go through your clothes. The first is to pretend you're shopping in a store. Pick up the item and ask yourself: Would I buy this right now at a store? How much would I pay for it? This should help you envision how you dress today, and let those items of clothing earn the first spots in your closet.

Another fun way to analyze whether or not to keep something is to ask yourself: How would I feel if I ran into my ex while I was wearing this? Those ill-fitting pants or stained shirt probably don't make you feel your most confident—so why keep them? Save yourself the discomfort or embarrassment of getting caught in the grocery store checkout line by that gossipy mom group chick and say adios to those ratty things. Sure, not every day is a fashion runway show, and I'm not saying give up your go-to comfies, but I am saying you should give priority to the clothes you feel most confident wearing.

You can also analyze what's in your wardrobe by defining your style. Defining your fashion style is like defining your home decor style. When it comes to my current house style, I have an eclectic midcentury maximalist vibe: cane chairs, lemon wallpaper, vintage radios, and stacked-up coffee table books. I love a boho nod with a sleek finish. Knowing this about my taste in home decor helps me be a critical shopper if I'm adding or changing any furniture or pieces in my house.

Use this same methodology to determine your fashion style so you can make better choices about clothing pieces you own, and to decide whether something should be retired or if new ones should be added. Not sure how to do that? Start by picking out your favorite outfit to wear—you know the one. You feel confident and comfortable, dressed up but ready to take on the world. Maybe you have two or three outfits that fit the bill. Make sure it's something you wouldn't mind being photographed in—this really shows how confident we feel in an outfit. Now that you have the two or three top choices, how would you describe their style? Pick three words to describe the outfit: is it chic, classy, modest, rock 'n' roll, vintage? What era does it favor? Is your spirit animal from the '70s your style, as evidenced by your bell-bottom preference, or is a '90s wide leg with pockets more your thing? What's your favorite thing about this outfit? You can use categories to describe this outfit, like "daily role," "work," or maybe even "alter ego." Describing your sense of style gives you a style cue card to compare to other clothes. This will help you purge what fits into your closet today and what doesn't. These days I'm an animal-print-lovin', rock-'n'-roll-vibin' casual CEO, so when I pulled out an old sweater the other day, I asked myself, "Would an animal-print-lovin', rock-'n'-roll-vibin' casual CEO wear this old blue Ann Taylor sweater that fits super tight?" The quick answer was no, which made it all the easier to toss in the donate pile. I have a bag in the spare closet at all times for any clothes ready to be textile recycled or donated—that way I don't hesitate to add to it instead of stuffing the clutter back in my closet knowing I'll never wear it.

Changing seasons presents a great opportunity to rethink what stays and what goes in your closet. As winter comes to a close I look over every sweater, jacket, coat, and sweatshirt. If I didn't wear it this season, then there's a good chance it moves to the donation bag. Again, just because it fits your body doesn't mean you're obligated to keep it. I promise you

you're not the only size 7.5 shoe wearer in the universe, so let that shit go if you don't wear it.

The closet is one of the most common places we find unused or unworn items. Gasp! A tag. Oh, the agony! As I said in the beginning: guilt and shame be damned. If you never quite figured out how to style that top or maybe once you got that dress home it didn't feel the same as it did in the store, so what? Occasionally you can recoup some of the value by selling on Poshmark or eBay, but be honest with yourself—the time you spend setting up, listing, and selling is precious time you may not be able to spare. Ask yourself if the Banana Republic factory dress you got for $28 is worth all that time you will spend trying to resell it online for maybe $8.

Finding the right avenues for donation is extremely important in this process. What we've seen with many clients is that sometimes knowing this avenue of donation is the ticket to being able to part with clutter. Whether it's a dress-for-success program or prom project, there's almost always a next home for your well-preserved item of clothing. Our all-time most popular blog is "Where to Donate in Houston"—check to see if there's something comparable where you live. From assistance ministries to shelters to school drives, there's always an avenue. If taking the time to research specific avenues isn't in your capacity, you can consider large nonprofit general donation centers such as Goodwill and the Salvation Army. (In Central Texas,

Goodwill funnels 94 cents of every dollar back into the local community, and they have a recycling process in place for items that don't sell in stores, making Goodwill one of the largest recyclers in the state.)

When determining the next life of an article of clothing, what you must consider before donating is whether the item can even be resold in a thrift store. If you wouldn't buy one sock or an armpit-stained tee, why do you think someone else would? That's where textile recycling comes in for those scraps of clothes that can no longer be worn. I make a drop almost every month to textile recycling bins, which are luckily in a few parking lots I frequent. It's an easy errand to add to the monthly list because there's always the snagged single socks, old T-shirts, or worn-out towels that can be made anew through textile recycling. In addition to the donation bag in my closet, I keep a bag to collect textile recycling as well. It seems that every load of laundry produces another addition to one of these bags.

Speaking of rotations, you might also consider a rotation system in your closet for seasonal swapping. This is useful when you have limited hanging space or dresser drawers. If the only direction to expand is up, using top-shelf space to hold the out-of-season clothes can make sense. This allows your current season to fill the easy-to-reach areas of hanging and drawers. Where I live in Houston, we have two seasons: *summer* for 10 months and *not summer* for the other two. Pajamas and workout wear are the two largest categories needing to be switched when the temperature outside changes.

Not to sound like a professor in a lecture, but let your closet space be your physical limitation to determine the most manageable size of your wardrobe. If you live with three roommates in Manhattan, bless your heart for even considering what an organized life could be for you. You're gonna make the most of that clothing rack, and you might consider stacked bins for seasons, since you actually have four of them in New York. For those who live in apartments or homes with average closets, this is your guide. Do I care if it means you use every closet in your house for your wardrobe? As long as it's categorized or arranged by season so you know which closet to go to when you're getting dressed, you do you, boo.

BATHROOM

Bathrooms can be sneaky clutter collectors. Most clients think that because the bathroom's square footage area is much smaller compared to the rest of the home, it must be incredibly faster to organize, right? After all, it's smaller than a kitchen or playroom. However, wrong-o you are. The bathroom has so many little, tiny things, so many different categories, and boy oh boy does it get dirty—because of its constant daily use and all the toiletries and hair products and makeup. Don't underestimate the amount of time needed to tackle this project just because the room is small.

NAKED2 BASICS
KEVYN AUCOIN
KEVYN AUCOIN
HEMP
LAVENDER
BECCA
BECCA
BEAUTYCOUNTER
BEAUTYCOUNTER
BROWFOOD | CLEAR BROW ENHANCING GEL FIX
BROWFOOD | EYEBROW ENHANCER
BEAUTYCOUNTER
Tint Skin Hydrating Foundation
jane iredale
NARS

DERMAdoctor

cotton
travel
toilet
Bandages & Wraps
Children's
Cold/Cough
Vitamins & Supplements
Cough & Cold
First Aid
Stomach
Pain & Prescriptions
Allergy & Skin Irritation
Kids Medicine
First Aid
Vitamins

As our personal care centers, bathrooms are the place we begin and end each day—which makes it an impactful space to organize. In doing so, you'll also be better at managing the inventory of your shampoo, toothpaste, and other frequently used toiletries. Talk about organizing a space with a great return on investment! No more overbuying inventory or forgetting what you bought on sale four months ago. This is an incredibly beneficial change needed for those of us (I'm looking in the mirror when I say this) who are easily swayed by the latest foundation collection release at Sephora that promises porcelain-smooth skin and a complexion worthy of a Hollywood star. It is also helpful when your toilet paper run to Target includes a browse through the beauty section overflowing with eye creams and lipsticks that somehow always seem like a pressing need the minute you pass. Nothing helps me run past this part of the store faster than knowing I have three more at home in unopened boxes—likely purchased during another low self-esteem episode. Remember the pandemic, when hair salons, spas, and personal grooming services of every kind were closed indefinitely and we convinced ourselves we'd learn how to apply gel polish, so we bought everything, including an array of color options that were maybe used once if we opened them at all? Anyone else? Just me? Cool, cool.

Back to organizing your bathroom. Because this area is constantly used and acts as a breeding ground for soap scum and hard water stains, it is a key area to deep-clean while organizing. After the Remove of ROAR is the time to do it—wiping down those drawers covered in hair and lotion leftovers while you're dragging all the products and other goodies out. Disinfectant wipes are your best friend in this space, because they make the cleaning part quick and thorough with one swipe.

One common tendency you may discover while organizing your bathroom is the urge to extend into your partner, spouse, or roommates' side. I will warn you now—as with any other intimate shared space, such as a closet, you must have their permission to mess with their stuff. If you don't have permission, save yourself the fight or the underlying resentment that will grow in someone who didn't want their shit messed with. My dude has had a dumpster fire of a sink area in our small, shared bathroom since we moved in, and you know what—it's really not a big deal, because he knows where his stuff is and it doesn't affect my routine one bit. Put your effort into the spaces that affect YOU and impact your daily routine. Leading by example is always the better route, and when your other half sees your stellar organized side, eventually the visual positive influence will rub off. Or it won't, because they're oblivious. Who knows? The point is, worry about the grass on your side of the fence. Even if that fence is invisible and you know what's in there.

Now on to the fun part! Let's unravel that disaster of a bathroom.

Using the ROAR method, we are going to remove every

single thing in your bathroom. No mascara left behind. Use your Post-its to identify categories as you remove #allthethings. After all items have been removed, move in for that hardcore wipe-down. You'll really see what yuck has built up, whether you've lived there one year or twenty years; these spaces get grimy quick.

It may be unnerving to see how many different types of concealers you have—especially considering you may only actually apply some twice a week—and how little backstock you have in deodorant. As you organize everything into categories, you may need to rehome certain categories altogether. One group that didn't belong in our primary bathroom was anything in the medicine/first aid category. Living in a one-story ranch-style home, it made more sense to combine this category and put all that belonged in it into the more accessible hall bathroom, the most central space in our home with the most storage space for it. The exception was daily vitamins, which moved to the pantry. This made sense because I always take these supplements with my breakfast and a large glass of water. (The one time I puked taking vitamins on an empty stomach has never left my memory and is definitely not a mistake to be made again.) Other categories you are likely to have in the bathroom include:

- **Dental.** Items here include extra toothbrush heads, toothbrushes for those who need a backup to the electric, toothpaste, floss, and tongue scrapers. Drawers are usually preferable for dental care.

- **Hair accessories.** This category will likely have subcategories of hair ties, hair clips, barrettes, bobby pins, headbands, bonnets, shower caps, and, thanks to an '80s and '90s fashion revival I pray is here to stay, scrunchies. In addition, you have the usual suspects of hairbrushes, combs, and for my comrades in the South, teasers. (We here in Texas say the higher the hair, the closer to God.) As an organizer, I say the higher the hair, the more hair crap you have in your bathroom. Hair accessories are better organized in a drawer or drawer-like setup, considering all the tiny pieces involved with clips and ties. You can mimic drawers with any kind of small stackable set found in most bathroom sections of your favorite store—or check out our professionally tested favorite products on our Amazon Storefront or LIKEtoKNOW.it app, all under Organized Life Design.
- **Hair care.** This category includes your styling prep products, hair spray, heat protectors, gels, creams, and dry shampoos. These types of products do not do well in drawers and, due to the height of some containers, may have limited options for their storage location. Under the sink is generally a tall area we look to first, unless you have a nearby upper cabinet within reach of your mirror area. Turntables with walls are perfect to store hair care so that you have

easy access, but also so things don't fall over when accessing them.

- **Hair tools.** Here we have your hair dryer, straighteners, curlers, and all stylers with a plug requiring an outlet to operate. Depending on your regular routine, you may keep your hair dryer separate and more easily accessible than the rest of your hair tools if that is something you use a couple of times weekly while the rest of the gang makes an infrequent monthly appearance. My hair dryer hangs at knee level on my bathroom vanity, as I'm likely to use it about once a week, while the others make only a semiannual appearance and are therefore tucked away in a drawer.
- **Shower toiletries.** Whatever you use in the shower is what belongs in the shower toiletries category: tour body wash, soap, shampoo, conditioner, and body scrubs. Think of this as your refill station to check first when you run out of product mid-suds.
- **Skincare.** Bring on the skincare routine. If you are a woman of a particular age, this is a broad and expansive category, from cleansers, toners, moisturizers, serums, and sunscreens all the way to masks, treatments, and possibly a few tools like rollers, gua sha devices, and cleansing brushes.
- **Grooming tools.** This category includes tweezers, scissors, trimmers, and face razors, which are vital for those of us sprouting beard hair or approaching our forties.

- **Disposable goods.** In this category we find cotton swabs, cotton balls, facial tissue, paper towels, toilet paper, and butt wipes. If you have a vulva, this may also include pantiliners, tampons, and other feminine care products.
- **Makeup.** Foundations, concealers, blushes, eyeshadow palettes, liners, lipsticks, glosses, brow shading, and mascaras all fall into the makeup category.
- **Nail care.** Nail polish, cuticle oils, nail clippers, nail files, cuticle trimmers, and polish remover.
- **Body care.** If it goes on your body, it goes in this group: lotions, creams, treatments, et cetera.
- **Towels.** All towels and washcloths used in this bathroom.

Now for the Analyze step of the ROAR process. Seeing these categories grouped will give you great clarity about what you own and allow you to make decisions on the right arrangement for your categories. I'm willing to bet you didn't know how many skincare products you had. This is one that always surprises me when I have to reorganize my bathroom every two to three years. Thanks to aging and hormones, finding the right routine seems to be an expensive puzzle. Expiration dates aren't as life-endangering as they are with food, but there is definitely a shelf life to toiletry products. Lotions will separate and mascara will breed bacteria—so open things up, check dates, and pretend you're at Sephora trying things on your hand and face. Most of us who wear foundation have more than one shade, depending on the season and how much sun we get. As with all analyzing processes, be ruthless. Who cares if you bought a Dior foundation if it makes you look like a ghost? If you feel insecure wearing it, I can promise you it's not worth keeping based on the price you paid for the bottle. Life is too short to walk around looking like you hired Donald Trump's spray-tanning specialist. The lipstick that makes you look washed-out and sick or the blush that doesn't last through your first meeting of the day—chuck 'em. Don't damage your self-esteem by wearing shitty makeup.

The guilt and torment you feel about the money you've spent is energy wasted on something you cannot change. You're making better choices moving forward, right? So forgive your brief error in judgment and let yourself move forward. Have dinner at home tonight instead of ordering Postmates—and just like that you've made up the $50 you spent on perfume that smells like sausages and grandma, so the budget discrepancy comes out in the wash. Samples are a common collection in many bathrooms, but they have a very short shelf life once opened. Toss any samples if you haven't used them a day or two after opening. If you have any new toiletries you can't use or don't want to use, shelters are a popular choice for donating these unopened items. As these projects progress, tasks will arise, like a donation drop. It's best to do the tedious errands and donation drops after each space organization project rather than waiting for it to pile up over the course of a month or year. Doing so will keep new clutter from accumulating, as well as build that get-stuff-done momentum. Reward yourself with a smoothie from your fave juice bar or some other treat after completing these mundane errands.

On to the Return portion of ROAR in this bathroom makeover, convenience is queen in a bathroom. It needs to be easy to brush your teeth when you're tired, do your morning routine quickly, or get ready for a date when you're already running late. (Who knew I could do a little Dr. Suess in an organizing book?) There is an ongoing debate about counters and whether you should keep any products on top or stash them all away, but I'm here to tell you it is essential to have easy access. And in a compact space, expanding to the counter may be your only choice. My current primary bathroom is the smallest I've ever lived with, but I'm also constantly in such a hurry that even opening and searching in one drawer is precious time I'm not willing to waste. I keep my daily skincare routine at arm's reach, because it's something I do twice a day. Feel free to also store your toothbrush, toothpaste, lotion, and deodorant in the easiest location to access, but give it structure with a mirrored tray or turntable so it doesn't appear like product just left out. It's definitely not necessary to rainbow-organize your product lineup or any category, for that matter, no matter how many insane TikToks you've viewed inspiring it. I am here to expose the truth: those people are not nurses, teachers, or accountants who are also getting kids ready for day care on a daily basis. In fact, I'd bet most don't even use the bathroom they are showing you but simply use it as a display for viral attention.

Assign a home for each category based on convenience and accessibility, which most of the time flows from the top of the counter to the bottom or back of the cabinet. There are a few occasions when splitting a category makes sense, and backstock (backup or extra of an item you use regularly) is one of them. While you know I love storing one category all together, it makes more sense to have my daily skincare routine on my counter and my restock skincare products in another area so that when I run out, I know where to check my inventory first.

This is true with almost every category listed in this space. You wouldn't have all your extra toothpaste in the same drawer; you'd keep your current tube in the top drawer, and the other few you have in a backstock spot. Use the physical limitation of how much you are able to store to determine how much you can actually store. This helps to prevent poor Costco decisions where you end up with way more toothpaste than you have space to store; it ends up living in three varied locations (one of which is forgotten), and you miss the point of saving money on the bulk buy because they aren't located again until they have expired.

If the pallet-sized case of toilet paper rolls is more than

your bathroom can hold, this professional is going to highly recommend you give up your big-box membership and opt for a package that actually fits in your space. We aren't in the pandemic, so we don't need to be hoarding any more toilet paper. If we learned anything from that, it's that no one in this country ever actually had a butt wipe emergency in 2020. Those days of frequent pandemic trips to Target to buy any cleaning product on the shelf even if you had eight more at home because you feared they would never be in stock again are behind us. Huzzah! Even into early 2023 we were helping clients who had stock purchased in 2020. We can now go back to our regularly scheduled programming of average household consumption.

Fold towels to maximize space. There are so many ways to fold, and some methods do appear neater than others. I always recommend folding based on what maximizes your storage area. If you have long, skinny cabinets, you're going to fold differently than if your cabinets are shallow and wide. (You can check out some of my favorite folding techniques on Instagram Reels.)

Label the categories so that even if you *Freaky Friday* switched with your kid's body, they could figure out what went where in your bathroom. (The new updated version of that classic movie, for those who don't know what I'm talking about, is *Family Switch* on Netflix with Jennifer Garner and Ed Helms, and it's precious and worth the watch.) Simple label tape is sufficient for the task of labeling your bathroom. Once your labeling is complete, take a moment to bask in your glory as you brush your teeth that evening, patting yourself on the back for a job well done.

While we as a team of professionals can tackle a bathroom in a day, don't be discouraged if it takes you a few days. It can be difficult to carve out enough time or summon enough energy to reach the finish line. Just stay laser-focused on one space at a time until it's done. Another name for organizers should be "finishers," because while it's so easy to start these projects, the true challenge comes in having the stamina to complete them all the way to labeled. If you're anything like me, it only takes a couple of trips out of town and a rushed getting-ready-for-a-night-out to wreak havoc on my organized bathroom. The good news is the reset is far easier with a foundational organized system in place.

BEDROOM

There's a reason this space isn't high on the list of most common spaces that need organizing. It's not that we don't find a number of cluttered abodes in our profession; more often, we find that the root of a messy bedroom is usually caused by clutter that bleeds over from other spaces. This is particularly true of the primary bathroom and wardrobe closet you use. Bedrooms are generally a collecting ground for laundry that hasn't been handled or clothes that don't fit. Maybe there are toiletries without a home there, or part of the bedroom has become the space where you store your items for restocking. Addressing those two spaces first and then coming back to what's left in the bedroom is a better order to reach feeling organized.

The dresser (if you have one) may need some attending to, and the nightstand might need a revamp, but outside of those two items, generally bedrooms don't house too many storage areas. A bedroom organization project can still make a huge impact, though, because this is the room where you first open your eyes in the morning and close your eyes at night—what a difference in your sleep and serenity to have this be a welcoming and calming space!

Feng shui, or the layout of the room, particularly in the bedroom where you lay your head each night, can be paramount to creating the serene environment needed for rest. Furniture layout and spacing in the bedroom make a huge impact on the flow of the room. When we first moved into our ranch house, we had an oversized bed with a huge headboard and footboard. The main bedroom wasn't huge: barely enough for a king-sized bed, a dresser, and two nightstands. If I had $5 for the number of times I jammed my mid-thigh on the corner of this giant footboard, I could have given this book out for free. It was sheer torture every time the lighting was remotely dim, particularly on a midnight bathroom run. I finally convinced my spouse to retire this ancient bed frame, and we opted for a more minimal headboard and skipped the footboard altogether. Do you know how many times I've thrashed an appendage on this bed frame? Zero times since replacing it! The right furniture and layout can make such a difference in comfort.

Finding the largest dresser to fit your space is better for long-term storage. Even if you can't fill it now, I have yet to meet someone who keeps a dresser empty for years. Like most pandemic survivors, my matching sweatshirt/sweatpant collection multiplied, replacing prepandemic clothes like jeans, and I'm happy we had a large dresser to accommodate all of it even if we didn't need all the space to begin with. Dressers can also serve as storage for jewelry and accessories like sunglasses and scarves, as well as bed linens.

Now let's talk "clerty clothes." This is a mix of the words "clean" and "dirty" to describe the items of clothing you wore for a couple of hours—the clothes you throw on for a run to the grocery store or to pick up the kids from school. You didn't sweat in them or spill anything on them, so they're not dirty enough to go in the hamper, but neither are they clean enough to be put back on a hanger or folded in the closet. These, my friend, are what I call "clerty clothes." Without a proper place for these clothes, they usually end up on your bed (shudder) and stay there until you kick them to the floor mid-REM cycle. In other instances, they are thrown on a nearby chair or bench or worst of all, **gasp** the floor!

What often happens is that the collection of clerty clothes

on the chair or bench grows and grows until what was on the bottom of the pile gets lost or forgotten. Sometimes the clerty pile becomes so large it resembles a mountain range and falls onto the floor. There are other options, *mis amigos*! One of my top choices is an extra-large hook to hang those worn-for-two-hour jeans or the pjs you'll wear for another night or two. What's great about finding a clerty clothes home spot is that it will help you keep these items visible so that you remember their existence—and as a bonus help decrease your laundry pile.

In fact, the outfit I'm wearing right now as I write this in the waiting room of my daughter's dance studio is something I wore for three hours a few days ago. It still smelled fresh, and I knew I could wear it again. Luckily the only person who saw me wear it the other day was my husband and kids, and they don't care (although I've totally shown up in the same outfit two days in a row for kids' pick-up, and they probably think I wore it for 24 hours straight, when in reality it was a clerty clothes revival).

My latest solution for clerty clothes is a small 12-inch hanging rack in the corner of the bedroom, as it combines a space shared by me and those in-between clothes—anywhere these clothes can stay visible as a reminder to wear them. What's great about a clothing rack is that you can use hangers, so it's super easy to maintain and stays looking neat and cute. Limit the number of hangers so it remains sleek and tidy.

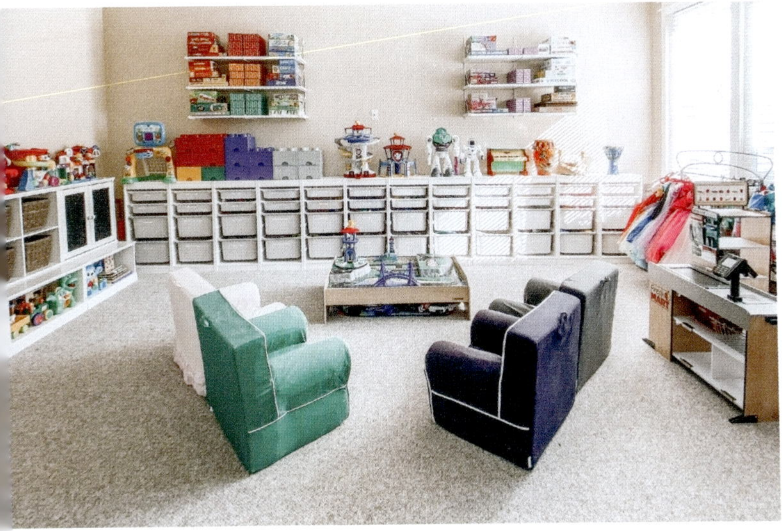

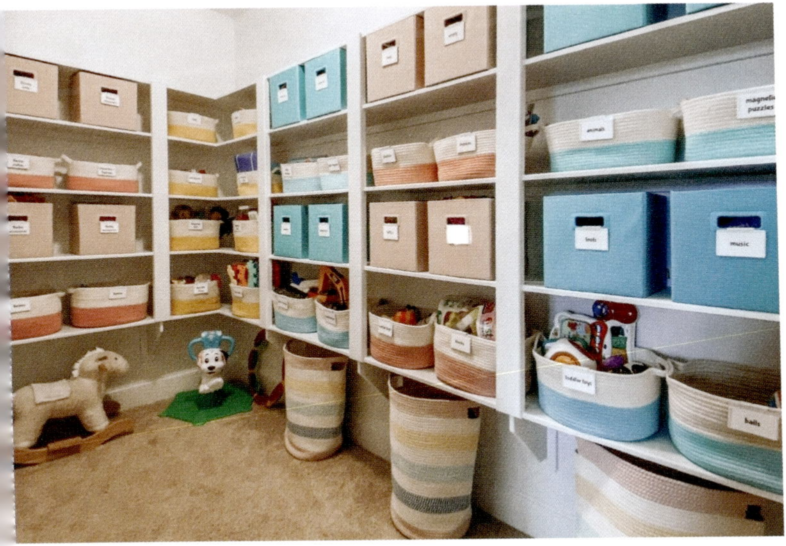
animals
puzzles
tools
music
toddler toys
balls

PLAYROOM

Good morning, Dolly Parton. If I could figure out a way to keep a playroom consistently clean and organized, I'd be a millionaire. Actually, I take that back: I do know two ways. The first is don't have any toys in there. I mean, talk about clean! But we all know that wouldn't go over well, so my second great idea is to hire regular help.

Okay, I'm kidding. Here's how you do it, including facing down the very real challenge of parental nostalgia and kid cooperation.

Every time I look at the mess and am ready to pull out the trash bags and get rid of it all, I remind myself that this is the only time they will be in this stage of imagination and play; in a few more years the only thing they'll want to play with is that stupid device with a screen that none of us can seem to get out of our hands. As we tell all our clients—and as I have to constantly remind myself in my own home—let your kids have access to as many toys as you are okay with having on the floor. That is the reality of toys. We can pretend they'll accept the self-responsibility of cleaning up, but I've learned from almost a decade of motherhood that this battle never ends with smiling faces. You feel like a nagging dictator and then have to spend an entire weekend getting it done yourself anyway. One thing you can try when they're really little is making a go at it when they're not home. Maybe they're in a Mother's Day Out program twice a week, or you can swap with a mom friend, where she watches the kids one day and then you watch them the next. Whatever works to give you the space to work through the playroom without tiny hands around. As they grow older, threats like deactivating the Wi-Fi if they don't clean up will help make it possible (I've totally done that, and it works 50 percent of the time).

Here are the tried-and-true methods that we've used with our clients (and that I try my best to use too).

Toy Rotation Systems

Using toy rotation systems is great with toddlers up through early elementary. It allows you to limit the number of toys that end up on the floor—and let's be honest, it's pretty much guaranteed that this will be the reality from the time they're six months old to at least six years. This method also renews your child's interest every few weeks when the current toy group is put away and the old toy group comes out again—it's like Christmas or a trip to Toys "R" Us on your birthday. These systems help them be less bored and save you from the creation of the disaster zone. Many preschools implement toy rotation systems for the same reasons—this week is dinosaurs, next week is trains kind of rotation. As your child grows, it may be tougher to limit entire categories, but I have learned that taking half the Barbie shit out of rotation helps prevent crippling chaos. The playroom should be constantly purged, and toy groups can be sold, retired, or donated.

An updated version of the toy rotation system is a breakaway from the traditional categories. If you have an imaginative kiddo who likes the farm animals to mingle with the Barbies and cross plays with these groups, then I wouldn't try to separate categories. The beauty of this is the Organize part of ROAR is simplified; instead, you're grouping the toy rotation systems based on what's on top of the pile until the bin is full. Then pull out the next bin and so on from there. Yes, your OCD tendencies may glitch, but this has proven to work for our little fashion designer and mini-inventor children. Embrace their play styles!

The good news here is that popular toy groups can easily be sold. One of my favorite ways to sell is the buy, sell, and trade local neighborhood group found on Facebook/Meta or Nextdoor. You assemble an entire toy group and sell it as a set if you can (when you can find all the pieces, or at least most of them). Lego also has an awesome donation program where you go to LEGO.com/replay and print out a label and ship all unwanted Legos back from a UPS store, and I highly recommend it.

Depending on the age of your child, maturity level, and general interest, it can be beneficial to include them in the purging process; this helps them see the results of the work and appreciate an organized life.

I make my kids participate in a deep cleanup of their rooms and playroom before Christmas every year in preparation for the incoming deliveries from Santa. This is a great teaching moment: "You don't play with this, sweetie, so why don't we donate to kids who don't have as many toys as you do. Wouldn't that be nice to make their day special?" If you have a kid who digs in their heels at this, remind them that they can keep everything—but then there won't be any room for new toys. We have to make space if we expect to fit new memories into our lives. This isn't something a two-and-a-half-year-old is going to grasp or even care about, so be sure to assess maturity for this conversation. If you're introducing this concept for the first time to an older kid, then you should also note that it will need repeating a few times before it's actually heard. Don't give up! Know it will plant a seed that could grow in a few months or a few years. This is a lifestyle change for you and your tiny humans. As with all spaces, store all the toys you can in the playroom, and anything that can't find a home there moves on, like the box of toys in *Toy Story*.

Letting Go

Many believe organizers are void of sentiment—able to toss in the donation pile on a whim—and that's simply not true. As I mentioned earlier, my daughter has given me permission to get rid of the toy kitchen set, but I'm not ready to let it go yet. There is no rule about how long I have to wait until I'm ready. There's no rule for you either. You may decide that even if an item is in the way, you still want to keep it—and I'm telling you it's okay. There is absolutely nothing wrong with holding on to a memory a little bit longer, even if it is taking up space. I don't think permission for this is talked about enough. Letting go is not a black-and-white activity.

CHILDREN'S BEDROOMS

Not much farther down the list, beyond the garages and playrooms, children's bedrooms can also be one of the most evolving spaces to organize. If this space also performs as a partial playroom, then you have doubled the challenge. Take heart, my friend. These are ever-changing spaces because kids are constantly growing, so their sizing is always in flux—from clothes to shoes to coats and everything in between. My number one organizing tip for these spaces is to keep one area for clothes they have outgrown and one for the clothes they haven't grown into. For the outgrown section you can set aside for donation or saving for your younger child or potential next child. Next, add in an area for clothes in the next sizes to be grown into. Keep both of these sections close by—like labeled bins on a shelf in the closet. This makes it easy: every time you put a load of laundry away, toss those outgrown clothes in. Equally as important, we want to keep the upcoming sizes close at hand so we don't forget to check as soon as that little one hits a growth spurt. Just this morning my oldest was hollering that none of her shoes fit—and she knew exactly where

DINOBLOCK
CORDUROY
romeo & juliet
MAMASAURUS
Pete Cat Meet Pete
All Better!
NOISY DINOSAURS
Good Morning, Good Night
THE CAT IN THE HAT
WAITING IS NOT EASY!
El camioncito Azul
Little Blue Truck
Little Blue Truck Leads the Way
SENSE & SENSIBILITY
PRIDE & PREJUDICE
COLORS
INSIDE OUT
Ravensburger
FEED THE WOOZLE
Mmmm! Yummy!
The Book With No Pictures
PLAYTOWN Roger Priddy
PHARRELL WILLIAMS HAPPY!
Adventure Tales
ENCYCLOPEDIA of DOGS
HAPPY BIRTHDAY TO YOU!
BIRDIE'S BIG-GIRL SHOES
Cinderella

to look for the next size up, which we'd stored in an underbed storage container, waiting on deck like a pinch hitter.

Books and Keepsakes

Books are another ever-changing category in your kids' rooms. Ledge shelves look aesthetically pleasing, but don't allow for a large quantity. In most cases a traditional bookshelf works. I'm fond of the cubby version, which acts as built-in bookends so the whole row doesn't topple over. I've seen kids' picture books stored as if they were vinyl records, in which books are in crates standing up and facing forward, letting you easily shuffle through them. This way of storing books does take up a lot of room, but it works really well with kids if you have the space.

I prefer keeping the kids' books in their bedroom over a playroom. Generally, that's where they're most often used. Storytime is big in our house, so it makes sense to have them stored near the beds. I've been a book nerd since the second grade, so getting rid of books is hard for me. The board books are very nostalgic: many of them are hand-me-downs, and by now you know my affinity for anything vintage.

Keeping a memory box for each child is important, too. The earlier you start, the easier it is to keep things organized. It could be filled with memories from trips, school programs, or birthday cards from Nonna—all those things are memories worth keeping. Turning their precious artwork into keepsakes is also a good idea, and there are many

ways to archive this, such as digitizing their art into coffee table books with a company like Artkive or Plum Print.

GUEST ROOM OR MULTIPURPOSE ROOM

If you're lucky enough to have a spare bedroom no one needs to sleep in on a regular basis—and don't need to use for a home office—a common flex is to turn it into a guest room. In my home, we rarely have guests, and with only two toilets, we're not all that eager to host. The spare room at the end of our hallway was up for grabs, and originally it was intended to be an office for my husband. Since he rarely works from home, the room went unused most of the time, so it was time to switch it up.

During the pandemic, the need to repurpose this space became apparent when my spouse and I separated (that's a story for another more personal book, but spoiler alert: we're back together), which meant I could use this room however I saw fit. Then I brought in a cycling spin machine. As one of the early buyers of the SoulCycle bike, I am forever a fan of the music-driven, high-cardio workouts I can do without leaving my house. This inspired me to create an entire workout space in part of this room. My library of books fit well in there and our collection has continued to grow, so another goal was to create a space where I could actually read all these books in a quiet area. Now you can find me there first thing most mornings meditating with my cup of coffee. This sanctuary also has the benefit of being one of the easiest places in my home to keep clean because I'm the only one in the house who uses it regularly. If I do find an unsanctioned pillow or Barbie doll, you can be sure I'm quick to pluck it out like a weed in a garden. I only wish we had this same discipline with the rest of our house!

If you're lucky enough to have this bonus space, don't be in a huge rush to assign it a function before you've tried out a few iterations. Sometimes these spare bedrooms become crafting spaces or music rooms with a collection of instruments. Or maybe you'll need this as a study room if you return to pursue a master's degree. All these functions will reveal themselves and therefore reveal the storage needed.

GARAGE

Lordy, the garage: also lovingly referred to as "exile," where everything you don't want in your house goes to die. The garage is where all the misfits from your life end up because you can't decide if you need it or if you can fix it. A garage is one of the dirtiest spaces we ever work in—full of bugs, spiderwebs, leaves, and dust.

Most garages challenge our clients to make tough choices about what items stay and what items go. Are you really going to fix that busted microwave, or is it time to find an appliance recycling center? Not to mention the vast to-do

O-Cedar

RESERVE PARKING
LONGHORNS
Blue Rhino

list of unfinished projects, from paint samples to broken furniture to every lightbulb type you've ever used. Rather than list a sampling of what could be in your garage, let's focus on the categories that belong there. Be ruthless with the unfinished projects in your garage. It can be tempting to keep those maybe-one-day-I-will items, but perhaps that day has arrived for someone else? Also, if it lasted through the pandemic and you still didn't get around to doing the project, chances are it isn't going to happen in the next five years either. Time to rip off the Band-Aid!

- **Tools.** This one is likely a duh, but your screwdrivers, hammers, power drills, nails, and everything in this category should have a designated area. You may just need a toolbox or a wall unit with a workbench and pegboard. There are many options for your garage setup depending on whether you refinish furniture or hang the occasional framed art piece.
- **Extreme weather event preparedness.** If you live near the Gulf Coast like I do—or anywhere else where hurricanes are a regular threat—this is what should be included in your hurricane box: a battery-operated or hand-crank radio, bottled water (at least one gallon per person), extra batteries, canned goods and other nonperishables, a flashlight, first aid kit and medications, a multipurpose tool, personal hygiene items, a cell phone with charger, personal documents, cash, family/emergency contact information, and extra

fuel for the car and generator. In other places where the weather may be extremely cold, you might also include hand warmers, tarps for vegetation, a whistle, blankets, and flares.

- **Sports equipment.** Considering we play many sports outside, the garage is a fitting place to store the basketballs, soccer balls, golf clubs, and more. You may choose to keep some equipment in a bag either in the garage or mudroom so it's easy to grab and go to practice. You should also have your bicycles in the garage with easy access for all family members. It's often too heavy or awkward to hang the front wheel at the top of the garage wall, so I encourage you to find a bike parking spot instead. The same goes for scooters and toddler push cars, where they move Flintstone-style using their own feet—make sure all these things stay accessible so the intended users are encouraged to use them often.
- **Gardening.** The garage is the place for various soils, garden tools, and plant pots.
- **Grill gear.** If you have a kitchen large enough to store your grill gear—fantastic! But since grilling happens outside, I deem the garage an acceptable location to store your gear and tools as long as you can protect them well from dirt and dust.
- **Pet products.** This is another category that may or may not need to extend to the garage, depending on

your inside storage. Extra food, treats, and supplies may be stockpiled here to unclog what is stored in the home.

- **Outside activities.** This could include picnic gear, beach gear, and bubble machines (which, by the way, are a racket; in my experience they last an average of 2.4 uses before never working again).
- **Folding chairs.** Whether needed for poker nights or watching soccer games, this is where the extra chairs can hang out.
- **Camping gear.** You won't find me near a campground anymore because I like hot showers and hate bugs, but many clients keep their trunks packed and ready for a weekend outdoor adventure with sleeping bags, lanterns, percolators, flashlights, camp stoves, grills, and tents. This honestly sounds too much like the extreme weather event preparedness category to me, which explains why I don't think you'll find me in a campground anytime soon.
- **Restock (inventory).** Depending on what you can keep in your home, this category may or may not be needed. If you can't store the 24 extra-big rolls of toilet paper inside the house, it's fine to store them in the garage—just keep them in the packaging until it's needed so as not to contaminate the rolls with all the dust and dirt the garage has to offer.

sides
sweets
eggs
eat me
bread
fruit
cheese
deli

TWEAKING

Tweaking is like twerking, but with less booty shaking—or the same amount of booty shaking—whatever you have to do to make this part fun. Don't we all wish that organizing was a one-and-done thing? I can't even paint a wall without thinking about the touch-ups that will be needed a few months later. The same adjustments are likely needed with any organized space. It may be one or two drawers of the bathroom or the kitchen, but it shouldn't be a purge of the entire room if we did the thorough ROAR process at the jump.

Tweaking happens when we realize a setup isn't working as smoothly as we hoped or because needs have changed—perhaps something isn't as accessible as it needs to be, or the product we used isn't the right fit after all. Our needs and interests do change: kids grow out of toy groups, or we retire an activity from our regular schedule. Give yourself a few days or maybe even a few weeks to feel out a newly organized space, especially a frequently used one. My pantry and bathroom are two of the most common spaces I tweak constantly—whether I change out products or preferences, a few alterations are needed every couple of months.

The playroom tweaking is the bane of my existence. Most weeks I can't for the life of me micromanage my children enough to keep it clean for long. When I do get through a reset, I've even locked them out for a few days just so I can admire the fact that it can be organized and in fact stay clean for longer than 10 minutes. Updating labels, discarding unused items, and switching up products is common. The goal and prayer I have for you is after you go through the full ROAR process in your spaces of concern is that tweaking is all that's needed a few times a year in any space.

All bets are off if you move, though, and you'll need to start all over.

GARY FISHER
TREK

Chapter 7

WHY AM I STILL NOT ORGANIZED?!

If you're lookin' for the soft-serve answer to this question, honey, look somewhere else. The following words will be full of tough love, but know this: we are in this TOGETHER. I don't just mean, "Oh babes, I got your back!" (I do!)—I mean that I am IN IT with you. Yes, I, a PROFESSIONAL ORGANIZER FOR A DECADE, am in it with you. Even as an expert in the very art form, I continue to grow each and every year. Pastors are sinners, chefs eat hot dogs, and I still have spaces in my home that challenge me in organization. I'm my own toughest client sometimes.

Writing this book and connecting with my clients in person and online makes me an even better professional organizer. I can absolutely relate to organizing challenges—a spouse who isn't on board, kids who disrespect their belongings on the reg, and dealing with a loved one's possessions after a funeral. I too am an Amazon Prime member and understand the ease of accumulation we have created for ourselves. As I read through this again, I realize I am my own worst enemy. We moved into our current home with a two-year-old and no savings. Over the course of nine years, things have certainly changed. We added another human, three more dogs, and extra hobbies including snowboarding, which requires a lot of gear! Living fully expansive lives comes with a little clutter, and I would choose it again for all the memories.

If you've learned anything from this book, I hope it's an understanding of how we got here—and I hope you can brush off some of that "I'm trash, it's all my fault" negative energy. The new goal is recognizing that when clutter is a problem that holds us back from living our best lives, we want to redirect that energy toward what will get us to the other side. Peace—freedom—calmness from the chaos. This book is a DIY but with the intention of healing ourselves first and foremost.

So WHY are you still not organized?! I'm willing to bet a huge sum of money it's one of the following reasons.

1. YOU'RE OUT OF ENERGY

I almost titled this section "laziness," but I truly don't think most of us are lazy; we're just FUCKING TIRED. We're permanently exhausted from keeping up with work, demands, responsibilities, and the scroll of obligations. At the end of the day, we just don't feel like putting our shoes back in their rightful home; they came off in front of the couch, and that's where they shall remain. We. Give. Up. The middle of your living room floor requires zero effort, and that's what we're plum out of—effort!

In these chapters of overwhelm, give yourself grace and maybe a hug too. You can't be perfect all the time. You're not Jesus, for heaven's sake! I'm here to tell you that it's okay: *it's completely normal* to have periods and seasons of less-than-perfect standards. Even chapters of dumpster fire standards. You're in your hot mess era, and this book will be waiting for you when things settle down.

2. YOU DON'T HAVE BUY-IN FROM YOUR ROOMMATES

If you happen to be related to your roommates, it will be a lot harder to evict them. Not having buy-in from your family to keep up with the organizing systems is a surefire way to grow tension and resentment. Living with a spouse who just doesn't care about how clean your pad is or a teenager who thinks you're the maid can hamper the results you seek. Perhaps multiple family meetings or even family therapy can help so you can all come to *understand* each other better and set reasonable expectations.

Remember, being an example first in your own spaces is the best place to start—it's where you have the most impact and control. Compromise will be key. Hopefully they'll make a little more effort in the shared living areas, and you'll be able to loosen the reins just a smidge, drill sergeant.

3. THERE'S NO SYSTEM

There's definitely a skill set involved when it comes to setting up an organization system. My goal in this book was to share some of those system-building skills, but it can take practice in several spaces to master. From the closet to the pantry to the garage, there's a science for figuring out why something goes where and how to organize it accordingly. In writing this book I've learned it's not the easiest to explain in words, like teaching someone how to paint using only words—a lot is learning by doing. Systems calculate accessibility, the space required to store versus space allocated to store, and the probability of being able to return to reset position. Like I said, it's an art form with a little math thrown in.

Remember that a passing grade is all that's needed. Make sure you're thinking not just about what looks good, but also what functions in your space considering your habits and lifestyle.

4. YOU HAVE AN OVER-ACCUMULATION PROBLEM

This one is gonna sting a little. And just to reiterate—I GET IT. It's so much easier to buy something than it is to find a home for it when it gets there. There are two ways to help overcome this epidemic of overaccumulation. The first is to be *ruthless* when deciding what to bring in to your home.

Use the acronym NOSE when you're considering what to bring in your home. Ask yourself these questions:

- **Now.** Do I need to use this right now today, or can it wait? Something being on sale right now is NOT a reason you need it right now today.
- **Own.** Is there something I already own that can get the job done well enough? Do I have a similar item that will suffice?
- **Someone else's.** Can I borrow this from a neighbor or friend? Can I rent this item?
- **Eliminate.** Can I eliminate the need for this item? This is where we analyze if what we are bringing in is solving a problem or whether we can eliminate the need. You may simply just want it, and I'm not your accountant or your parent. We just want to be sure we'll have a home for this item when it gets here.

These NOSE questions apply to everything from groceries to new clothes to toys for your kids. They invite internal dialogue to help you maintain your organized home.

5. YOUR LIFESTYLE NEEDS AN ADJUSTMENT

I was going to say "reality check," but adjustment sounds less aggressive. Read this twice: the more things you own, the more time you will need to manage those things. The fewer things you own, the less time and energy spent managing those things. It is a truth I have preached over the years. You can own as many things as you want—just know it will take time to manage each and every single item.

If you spent just 10 minutes a week handling an item you own—using it, moving it, putting it back—that adds up to over eight and a half hours PER YEAR. Say what?! You read that right. A full workday can be spent on a pair of shoes or a broom. Knowing this can help you become more protective about what you bring into the sanctuary of your home. Be guarded against items that don't serve you or your family.

Another element of your lifestyle that could be curtailing your organizing dream is the fact that you fill every waking hour you can with work, events, and activities and end up back to point *numero uno* on this list. This overscheduling doesn't even allow you the time to unpack your day and reset for the next morning, which invites the clutter monster to appear.

Did I mention that I can relate to EVERY SINGLE NUMBER on this list?

Homie, this is not me wagging my finger at you. If I was wagging my finger, I'd also be wagging it at myself in a mirror. The challenges you face are relatable and common. Acknowledging and understanding these hurdles and determining which are the toughest for you will be the catalyst you need to finally design your organized life!

Conclusion

FREEDOM

There are two scenarios in which you should give clutter the middle finger. Scenario A is when today is not the day you are able to deal with it. That pile of shit you don't have time for can take a back seat, like back-of-the-yellow-school-bus kind of back seat. You have too many obligations to deal with, or you've hit a freaking wall and have reverted to survival mode. Whatever the case may be, you're allowed to say "fuck you, clutter" and ignore it . . . until you are ready. Scenario B is when you are ready, finally ready to stop letting the mess control your life and hinder you from reaching personal and professional goals. You're ready to kick it to the curb and make a change. The fed-up

meter is to the top, and there's a fire in you to make it happen. Your realm of doom is over, clutter! Hit the road, and don't let the door hit ya where the good Lord split ya. Fuck off. Both of these are appropriate times to give clutter the middle finger at different chapters in your life. Heck, I feel both of these vibes in the same week sometimes.

Remember our goal of getting organized? *Freedom*. The whole point of getting organized is finding freedom—in your schedule, in your spaces, and in your mental bandwidth. You should come home and feel at home, not tortured by clutter screaming your name for attention. If you're in Scenario B, it's time to stop stressing about clutter and get back to doing the things you love the most in life.

Don't forget—being more organized isn't a visual goal. It's a feeling you have about how you are managing your own life. Can you find what you need when you need it? Boom, you're organized. There is little in this world over which you truly have influence, but you do have influence within the four walls where you live. Notice I didn't say you have complete control, but you do have influence. Even if you live alone, while you may not have family members or roommates to contend with, the expectation of maintaining a perfect home is an incredibly high standard to keep for yourself. If you finished top of your class in college, maybe nothing but the top slot feels right to you. For the rest of us average students, I release you from trying to make an A and settle for a passing grade.

Here's what I know to be true. When my house FEELS organized, I'm a more involved mom, a more doting and nurturing spouse, and an all-around less frazzled human being. Maybe you've been trying to reach your organizing goal for years or maybe this is the first book on organizing you've ever been interested in picking up. Either way, I'm here to cheer you on and guide you through the process. And if all you do is give that laundry pile the bird and gift yourself with an early bedtime, then, friend, I'm also here to applaud you for showing up and doing the best you could today. Who knows what tomorrow can bring?

Finally, I just want to say that one of the qualities I'm most excited about for this book is the access to me—my favorite professionally tested products and several tutorials and videos mirror all the skills shared in this book, and I'm happy to share more. I encourage you to use all these amazing reference tools to help along your journey. You can find me on Facebook, Instagram, YouTube, TikTok, and Pinterest.

@organizedlifedesign
/organizedlifedesign
www.organizedlifedesign.com

You've tackled a huge hurdle by learning so much in this book—applause for that! I would love to hear how your journey is going, your challenges, and your wins.

ACKNOWLEDGMENTS

First and foremost, I want to thank God for saving my ass time and time again. Without God's grace and mercy, I can't imagine where life would have taken me. All my courage, resilience, and belief in myself come from Jesus and my fervent conviction in Jesus's teachings. May I continue to learn from You, walk with You, and be more like You every day of my life.

Thank you to my mommy, Vivian. Without your love for my sister and me, I would not be the woman I am today. You made so many sacrifices to be there for us, and your actions are not unnoticed. I am grateful you raised me to be a kind, empathetic person who seeks justice in the world even when it is heartbreaking. You are a wonderful grandmother to my girls, which has enriched my love for who you are as a person. I love you, Marmie!

Thank you to my husband, Salvatore, who, right after Jesus, is my favorite man to walk this Earth. This book would not exist without your encouragement and financial contribution to the process, allowing me to write it. We have been through a series of unrelenting life storms that could have broken us at any turn, but here we still stand, choosing our love for each other again and again. Your bravery and humor fill my cup every single day. I love you so very much, bear.

Thank you to my daughters, Sophia and Lucia, who give me so much happiness and headaches. Being your mom is one of the most important roles I will ever have, and I am honored to witness the amazing, voracious, and creative women that you are becoming. I pray that you will know what love and kindness feel like and that you become agents of goodness in this crazy world. You are each half of my heart, and I love you to the moon and back.

Thank you to all who have worked alongside me at Organized Life Design. I am so thankful for your trust in me and for sharing your love for organizing with our clients! Miriam, I am beyond grateful for you; Organized Life Design would not have reached the success it has without you. This book could only happen with you at my side, and the friendship that has formed over the years will always be special. I truly hope you know what a godsend you have been to my life through all the ups and downs. Michelle and Brittany, your energy and laughter will always be a light. You have been amazing teammates and, I am honored to say, friends who continue to encourage me in this new chapter of life.

Thank you to my sister, Melanie. You are my Rory and my forever ride-or-die. You make me crazy, you make me laugh, you make me feel sorry for anyone who doesn't have a sister like you in their lives. Thank you for your faith in me, for supporting me, and for always being there for me. I love you so very much, sissy.

Thank you to many friends who have supported me over the years.

Thank you to Allison and Kelly, who listened to the ideas of this book begin to form during the pandemic. You became my first audience for this message and gave me the confidence to put pen to paper. I am grateful for your friendship and encouragement.

Thank you to Ally, who knew that a first-grade date to play paper dolls and Barbies would turn into a lifelong friendship that has stood the test of time. You might know me better than anyone else on this planet, and the fact that you still want to be my friend means I might be kinda cool. Your support and encouragement over the years have brought me through so many low spots, and I am delighted to share this high point with you and tell you how much I love you, my dear friend!

Thank you to Bri, my mama friend, meme sister, and favorite running partner! You know a true friend when she holds your hair while you puke your guts out and gets you safely to the ER at 4:00 a.m. when you have inexorable food poisoning. Your friendship gives me so much hope and cheer. Love you, friend!

Thank you to Paige and Sue—you have held space for me in my latest chapter of life, which has been a blessing more than you know. Just being you, as you exist in the world, being a part of your journey, has given me so much inspiration. As I embark into this next phase as a budding author and future pastor, I am most grateful to be on this path alongside two of the bravest, most compassionate people I have ever met.

Thank you to my publisher, Greenleaf, and the team for not giving up on me. Dee, Leah, and especially Tess, thank you for sticking by me through this process. Life kept "life-ing" as it tends to do, and through hurricanes, two rounds of COVID, the flu, pneumonia, moving adventures, chronic illness flares, water-damaged ceilings falling through, and many other fun happenings in the last year, I appreciate your encouragement and support to bring this heartfelt creation to life.

Finally, to my dogs, Lil Jon and Biggie Smalls. All the shit and piss you leave in my house is forgiven because of how much joy and comfort you bring me. On the lonely days of healing chronic illness flares or questioning my existence in the world, you have licked my face and cuddled in my lap, loving me just the way I am. You are my truest example of unconditional love, and though you can't read and won't know I'm writing this, I promise to keep giving you treats and taking you on walks as a sign of my gratitude. I love you, my sweet boys.

ABOUT THE AUTHOR

MEGGIE MANGIONE is an accredited professional organizer and has been the owner of the organizing services company Organized Life Design in Houston, Texas, for over ten years. Meggie has shared her obsession with organizing at the organizedlifedesign.com blog as well as being featured in print and online with *Domino*, *Real Simple*, the Food Network, and Houzz. She runs on '90s alternative rock music, morning coffee, Jesus's teachings, half marathons, and quality time with loved ones. Meggie lives with (**ahem**)—cleans up after—one loudmouthed Italian husband, Sal; two strong-willed, hilarious daughters, Sophia and Lucia; and two stubborn, joyful dogs, Lil Jon and Biggie Smalls.

Photo by Stacy Sikes